Gender Budgets Make Cents

Understanding gender responsive budgets

Debbie Budlender, Diane Elson, Guy Hewitt
and Tanni Mukhopadhyay

Gender Affairs Department
Commonwealth Secretariat
Marlborough House
Pall Mall,
London SW1Y 5HX
United Kingdom

E-mail: gad@commonwealth.int
http://www.thecommonwealth.org/gender
http://www.gender-budgets.org

Published by the Commonwealth Secretariat

Layout design by Wayzgoose
Cover design by Pen and Ink

Copies of this publication can be ordered from:
The Publications Manager, Information and Public Affairs Divisions,
Commonwealth Secretariat, Marlborough House, Pall Mall,
London, SW1Y 5HX, UK
Tel. +44 (0) 20 7747 6342
Fax. +44 (0) 20 7839 9081
E-mail: publications@commonwealth.int

ISBN: 0-85092-696-3

Publication Team

Coordinator: Guy Hewitt

Contributors: Debbie Budlender, Diane Elson, Guy Hewitt and Tanni Mukhopadhyay

Editor: Tina Johnson

About the Contributors

Debbie Budlender: Debbie Budlender is a Principal Researcher for the Community Agency for Social Enquiry (CASE), Cape Town, South Africa. A founding member of the South African Women's Budget Initiative, she is the leading international adviser on gender responsive budget (GRB) initiatives, having worked in Africa, Asia, the Caribbean, Europe and the Americas. She has also written extensively on this area.

Diane Elson: Diane Elson is a Professor in the Department of Sociology at the University of Essex, UK. She has written numerous books and articles on gender equality and economic life. She was responsible for *Progress of the World's Women 2000*, the UNIFEM biennial report, and co-editor of a special issue of the *World Development* journal (July 2000) on Growth, Trade, Finance and Gender Equality. She advised the Commonwealth Secretariat on the development of the expenditure tools for the GRB initiative and UNIFEM on the implementation of its global programme on gender responsive budgets. She is also a member of the UK Women's Budget Group.

Guy Hewitt: Guy Hewitt is a Senior Programme Officer in the Gender Affairs Department at the Commonwealth Secretariat, and programme manager of the Commonwealth GRB initiative. He advises Commonwealth governments on the implementation of gender responsive budgets and also provides technical support to other intergovernmental organisations and developmental agencies.

Tanni Mukhopadhyay: Tanni Mukhopadhyay is a Policy Specialist in the Human Development Report Office at the United Nations Development Programme (UNDP), New York. She has worked as a researcher with the University of Cambridge and with the Commonwealth Secretariat on its GRB initiative. She has also worked with, and conducted research on the Self Employed Women's Association (SEWA) in India and the Population and Community Development Association (PDA) in Thailand. Her main areas of research have been on poverty, trade policy and market access issues.

Contents

Foreword

The involvement of Commonwealth countries in gender responsive budgets is both long and substantial: it began with Australia in 1984 and spread to Canada and South Africa in 1993 and 1994, respectively. The Commonwealth Secretariat's programme began in 1995 and since then nearly half of the forty known country initiatives on gender responsive budgets are in the Commonwealth. The issue has been discussed in depth at the Fifth and Sixth Meetings of Commonwealth Ministers Responsible for Women's Affairs and it was on the agenda of the September 2001 Commonwealth Finance Ministers Meeting which, like a number of other international meetings, was cancelled following the tragic events in the USA.

The Commonwealth's involvement in gender responsive budgets takes its genesis from a number of discreet but interconnected factors:

- The Commonwealth's commitment to the fundamental principle of equality and non-discrimination, first affirmed in the 1971 Singapore Declaration and reaffirmed in the 1991 Harare Declaration, which creates the need to develop public expenditure tracking systems to measure how consistent national decisions on resource allocation are with these and the other fundamental principles of the Commonwealth.

- Reaffirmation of the commitment to gender equality by Heads of Government when they endorsed the *Ottawa Declaration (on Women and Structural Adjustment)* at Harare in 1991, the 1995 *Commonwealth Plan of Action on Gender and Development* and its 2000–2005 Update in 1999.

- Exploitation of the Commonwealth's comparative advantage in the area of encouraging governments to integrate gender concerns into economic policy dating from the report of the 1989 Commonwealth Expert Group on Women and Structural Adjustment, *Engendering Adjustment for the 1990s,* a pioneering work that advocated incorporating gender concerns into a broad range of economic policy areas: public expenditure, taxation, credit policies, exchange rate policies, pricing policies, wage policies, trade liberalisation and privatisation.

Gender Budgets Make Cents provides the conceptual framework for the Commonwealth's work on GRB initiatives, the outcomes to date of work in the Commonwealth and beyond and an assessment, based on practical experiences, of what has worked. The contributors draw on initiatives that have been undertaken at national, provincial and local levels. This publication will be of use to anyone interested in strengthening the linkages between economic policy and social outcomes. It is our hope that it will be used by government officials, policy-makers and planners, multilateral and bilateral agencies and civil society groups, especially women's organisations.

The work done by the Gender Affairs Department in the area of gender responsive budgets has been a collective effort among many individuals and groups. Their contributions to the conceptualisation and implementation of this programme are gratefully acknowledged. In particular, I wish to thank the following: the Commonwealth member countries who have sought to implement gender responsive budgets, especially the five 'pilot' countries; Commonwealth Ministers Responsible for Women's Affairs for their leadership; the Commonwealth Fund for Technical Cooperation (CFTC) for funding this work and also the Department for International Development (DFID) and the Australian Agency for International Development (AusAID) for their contributions to this programme; Debbie Budlender, Diane Elson and Rhonda Sharp, our primary consultants and subsequent friends, for their continuous involvement and invaluable inputs; colleagues in the Commonwealth Secretariat, especially Ranee Jayamaha; and the staff of the Gender Affairs Department (including Eleni Stamiris and Sabhita Raju), particularly Guy Hewitt, the programme manager, who has coordinated this work from its inception. Finally, I would like to recognise the significant contributions of our new programme partners: the International Development Research Centre (IDRC) and the United Nations Development Fund for Women (UNIFEM).

This publication is part of the Commonwealth's contribution to the global agenda of attaining gender equality and the Commonwealth vision of 'a world in which women and men have equal rights and opportunities at all stages of their lives to express their creativity in all fields of human endeavour'. We hope that it will provide inspiration and guidance to those already involved in or considering work on gender responsive budgets.

Nancy Spence
Director, Gender and Youth Affairs Division
Commonwealth Secretariat

Executive Summary

This publication was compiled to provide the reader with a comprehensive understanding of gender responsive budget (GRB) initiatives. Divided into four sections, it provides a conceptual and theoretical framework, traces the evolution of work in this area, assesses the role of different stakeholders and highlights lessons learned to date. A profile of known activities at the country level shows how gender responsive budgets are being used as a pivotal tool with which to assess budgetary performance and impact.

GRB initiatives are intended to afford a mechanism by which governments, in collaboration with lawmakers, civil society groups, donor and other development agencies, can integrate a gender analysis into fiscal policies and budgets. A gender responsive budget is not a separate budget for women but an attempt to disaggregate expenditure and revenue according to their different impacts on women and men.

The idea of gender responsive budgets developed out of a growing understanding that macroeconomic policy can contribute to narrowing or widening gender gaps in areas such as incomes, heath, education and nutrition and make the living standards of different groups of women and men better or worse. The Commonwealth Secretariat played a pioneering role in fostering this understanding in its work on women and structural adjustment. One of the most important areas of macroeconomic policy is a government budget. Bringing together public expenditure and public revenue, the budget as a policy statement reflects the social and economic priorities of a government. Although the provisions in a budget may appear to be gender netral, they actually affect men and women differently because their roles, responsibilities and capacities in any society are never the same.

In her contribution, Diane Elson argues that national budgets generally underestimate women's contribution to the macroeconomy, discount the unpaid economy in which women perform most of the work of caring for and maintaining the

Programme Objectives of Gender Responsive Budget Initiatives:

- *To strengthen the capacity of governments to incorporate a gender analysis in the planning and evaluation of revenue-raising measures and expenditure allocations at all levels;*
- *To support strategies for women's participation in economic decision-making through their engagement in the budget process;*
- *To improve the mechanisms used by countries to account for action taken on international commitments to gender and development, including the CEDAW; and*
- *To contribute to the achievement of the International Development Targets (IDTs).*

labour force and the social framework, and disregard the effect that gender relations and the gender distribution of resources have on total production, savings, investment, etc.

Elson points to the economic costs of gender inequality and the growing awareness that such inequality is not only costly to women but to society as a whole. Research has shown that gender inequality reduces agricultural yields, hampers a positive supply response to structural adjustment measures and reduces the productivity of the next generation. Also, failing to invest in female education lowers the gross national product (GNP). On the other hand, eliminating gender discrimination across occupations and in salaries and benefits increases not only women's income but also national income. Other potential gains to society from the reduction of gender inequality include greater output of goods and services, more leisure, increased capability to live a satisfying life and better conservation of the environment.

There is also an increasing recognition that macroeconomic aggregates (and national economic prosperity) do not, as had been assumed, have a 'trickle down' effect. Rather, governments need to explicitly consider human development objectives when formulating macroeconomic policy. Elson contends that gender responsive budgeting can make such policy design more effective as it contributes to the reduction of gender inequality, and hence reduces gender constraints to successful macroeconomic outcomes. This improves economic growth and human development performance in ways that also empower women.

Elson notes that the formulation of a national budget involves decisions at three levels: aggregate macroeconomic strategy, composition of expenditures and revenues, and effectiveness of service delivery. She offers a wide range of analytical tools for the integration of a gender perspective into these different levels, with an emphasis on public expenditure. These tools can be used individually or in combination and selected according to national circumstances.

When looking at the effectiveness of public expenditure, which is usually judged in terms of achieving the intended results at the lowest possible cost, a gender perspective introduces the questions of 'results for whom?' and 'costs to whom?' Some ways of addressing these questions include needs assessments, analysis of 'quality of service' indicators, beneficiary assessments, assessments of 'invisible' costs and assessments of benefits of equal opportunities in service delivery. Elson emphasises that indicators need to be disaggregated by gender in all these cases.

Expenditure and taxation policies have different implications for women and men and differentially affect their abilities to contribute to production for the market and the care of families and communities. These implications can be revealed through gender-disaggregated incidence analysis of public expenditure and of taxation and income transfers. An analysis can be made of the share of the budget that goes to the Ministry Responsible for Women's Affairs compared to other ministries, and gender-aware policy appraisals can be applied to facilities and policies of Ministries that provide collective services. Another important tool, which can bring together information on the implications of government expenditures for women, is a women's budget statement.

A GRB strategy might also include examining women's critical role in maintaining the social framework through the unpaid work that they do bringing up children to be responsible members of society, looking after the elderly and infirm, and strengthening family and community networks and voluntary organisations. Monitoring the time budgets of the country's citizens can show whether the human resources of women and girls are being depleted by the demands of unpaid work, damaging the social framework and leading to reduced productivity and increased costs. The development of gender-aware medium-term economic policy frameworks is another valuable tool.

Decisions on budget policy are usually made by a small group of Ministers and officials in the Head of Government's Office, Ministry of Finance and/or Central Bank. To improve the efficiency gains and equity outcomes, Elson recommends that these Ministers and officials should collaborate with the Ministry Responsible for Women's Affairs and civil society groups. The Commonwealth Secretariat has already taken measures to facilitate such interaction by submitting reports on the gender impacts and macroeconomic policy issues to the meetings of Commonwealth Finance Ministers and Ministers Responsible for Women's Affairs, and through its partnership with IDRC and UNIFEM.

Like Elson, Guy Hewitt and Tanni Mukhopadhyay in their contribution point to the increasing recognition that economic growth is a necessary but not sufficient condition for the elimination of inequalities in society. State intervention in the market is thus needed to ensure that both efficiency and equity objectives are met, and gender responsive budgets can assist in this process. The authors provide a conceptual framework for GRB initiatives, suggesting that public expenditure for gender equality fits within a wider context of promoting economic growth and supporting social inclusion and human resource development. While GRB initiatives differ across countries and regions, the Commonwealth Secretariat has focused on an analysis of government expenditure in three categories: gender specific expenditures; expenditures that promote gender equity in the public service; and general or mainstream expenditures.

Hewitt and Mukhopadhyay argue that there are compelling reasons to ensure greater consistency between economic goals and social commitments and thus for undertaking GRB initiatives. The rationale most often put forward is the efficiency gains, since gender analyses improve targeting and result in a more optimal use of limited public resources. Gender responsiveness is also a key feature of good governance which the authors argue, as it promotes participation, accountability and transparency, is a prerequisite for and essential component of sustainable human development. GRB initiatives further these processes of facilitating more open government since they foster dynamic and active partnerships with civil society groups, especially women's organisations, encourage the use of gender-disaggregated data in planning and evaluation, and improve the reporting on the social impacts and outcomes of government actions.

GRB initiatives also assist governments in fulfilling their commitments to international agreements and Commonwealth mandates. They build on the global consensus on the priority of gender equality, and are a practical application of gender mainstreaming, the current international approach to promoting equality between women and men.

The nature of GRB initiatives varies from country to country, and they have been undertaken at national, provincial or local levels. Some were coordinated and led by governments, others by civil society groups. Hewitt and Mukhopadhyay examine the role of different country-level actors and some of the strategies used, providing examples from Commonwealth country experiences. The Ministry of Finance, for example, has a key leadership role for several reasons. The participation of the Ministry Responsible for Women's Affairs is also central. The whole process needs to secure political support from the highest levels of government. Lawmakers also have an important role to play, either through participation in debates or their powers to amend budgets, and civil society should be fully involved.

The authors bring out some of the lessons learned from gender responsive budget analyses and processes, identifying a number of opportunities as well as challenges. The positive benefits that have emerged include an enhanced ability to determine the real value of resources targeted towards gender-specific groups; the challenge to notions of 'gender-neutrality' of many policies and programmes; and the strengthening of the collection and analysis of gender-disaggregated data. They then offer suggestions for strengthening GRB initiatives for implementation on a wider scale, supported by the Commonwealth Secretariat and its new inter-agency partners, the International Development Research Centre (IDRC) and the United Nations Development Fund for Women (UNIFEM). Future programme directions include improving the efficacy of GRB initiatives as part of a strategy to increase collaboration between governments and civil society groups, increase the access of vulnerable groups to resources, goods and services, and improve the rate and distribution of the benefits of economic growth. Tools for revenue analysis also need to be developed that look at direct and indirect taxation and at user financing of basic social services.

Debbie Budlender has contributed two sections to this publication. The first is a global assessment of gender responsive budget initiatives, while the second provides a profile of country activities. Having been directly involved in GRB initiatives in more than 15 countries, Budlender is able to offer an overview of how the goals and objectives of the initiatives differ from country to country and illustrate the diversity of activities that have taken place under this heading.

In the global assessment, Budlender explains that the budget has proven a useful place to start work on engendering macro-economic policy because gender concerns are more visible in fiscal policy than in monetary policy. Since budgets have an annual cycle, this focus also allows the processes of analysis, problem identification, implementation of corrective measures, and monitoring and evaluation of impacts to be completed within a relatively short time. Further, GRB initiatives can be implemented at the country level with a relatively small amount of resources.

The goals and objectives of GRB initiatives differ according to country and the particular stakeholders' interests. One advantage of having varied objectives is that these initiatives appeal to a broad range of actors many of whom would not normally be concerned with gender issues; finance and budget officials are targeted and engaged in a practical way allowing them to understand and respond to issues of gender inequality.

Like Hewitt and Mukhopadhyay, Budlender stresses that there are many potential players in GRB initiatives at the country level. Her recommendation is that, where possible, these initiatives should try to involve all those who can have a significant impact on making government budgets more responsive to gender concerns. The government has been the main focus of the Commonwealth Secretariat initiative and Budlender notes that, along with the Ministry of Finance and Ministry Responsible for Women's Affairs, other ministries such as health, education and agriculture have often played a significant role. The support of senior officials in these sectors thus needs to be gained. It is important for GRB initiatives to target the bureaucracy as well as the legislature in order to change budget policy and outcomes since the budget has usually been finalised by the time it is presented to parliament.

Civil society participation in GRB initiatives is facilitated by a broad common purpose of actors inside and outside government. From within civil society, it is usually NGOs who take the lead. According to Budlender, these NGOs are often comprised of women who are contemporaries of those in government, which facilitates greater collaboration. Men have also played a significant role and featured as the 'target group' for lobbying and training in government initiatives because of the dominant role they play in budgetary decision-making. Some of the initiatives have drawn on academics and research institutions to assist with the research, or even training. Apart from institutions, strategically-located individuals have also been extremely important in ensuring the achievements of the more successful initiatives, although Budlender warns against reliance on individuals in case the initiatives are not carried through when these 'champions' are no longer around.

Research can play an important role in GRB work. It needs to be sophisticated enough to convince those with technical knowledge, while being simple enough to be understood by less technical gender advocates. Most gender responsive budget analysts complain about having too little information, particularly gender-disaggregated data, but even limited information can be useful for advocacy and mobilisation. On the other hand, there can also be a problem of having too much data, particularly when most of it is not organised in a form that is useful for analytical purposes.

A number of analytical tools for budgetary expenditure analysis are outlined by Budlender, as well as several basic frameworks which, with variations, have served as the basis of many exercises to date. Some GRB initiatives, especially those not undertaken by government, have focused on the budget process itself. An understanding of this process can help identify places where particular groups of actors can have an impact and should be involved. It may also reveal that there is a lack of communication between those responsible for the various steps involved in developing and implementing budgets. This situation can sometimes be helped through workshops that bring the different groups together.

Budlender underlines the importance in any workshop of acknowledging and respecting participants' knowledge as well as of providing the opportunity for participants and facilitators to learn from each other. Almost all GRB initiatives include some element of training or capacity building for researchers, for different types of advocates and for government officials. Such training, especially when directed at government officials, needs to provide clear guidelines and methodologies and be located within a wider implementation strategy and capacity building process. She notes that where training has been organised without the purpose, target group and follow-up being clearly identified, it has proven to be unsatisfactory for both organisers and participants. Since the resources available to support gender and other developmental programmes are limited, it is vital to be clear as to the objectives, strategies and processes of all planned activities.

In terms of international donor participation in GRB initiatives, Budlender notes that a number of multilateral and bilateral agencies have provided support. Sometimes, however, the specific departments involved have reported opposition from their colleagues, particularly from those in the economic affairs sections. Also, the support may be limited in terms of scope and actors. In several countries, there are reports of misunderstanding and even opposition to introducing gender into discussions of macroeconomics, or even poverty reduction strategies. Where gender is introduced, it may only be in a limited way. International NGOs and development agencies are more likely to fund initiatives that focus on civil society, as some bilaterals have been restricted by their need to obtain permission from the governments prior to providing support to NGO activities.

One of the drawbacks of donor support is financial dependency and the dangers this poses to the sustainability of the project. Budlender notes that there is also some opposition among both governments and NGOs to donor-driven initiatives. Because of the necessity of country ownership, and since GRB initiatives are also about (self) governance and democracy, the author notes that the Commonwealth Secretariat, IDRC and UNIFEM prefer to support initiatives that have been planned and are being undertaken at the country level rather than initiating action.

Several countries have also initiated gender responsive budgets at the sub-national level and Budlender believes that there should be more work at this level. She suggests that local level interventions make sense given that many countries are increasingly decentralising administrative functions and budgets. However, she recommends keeping in mind that, in many countries, national leaders tend to be more aware of and sensitive to gender equality issues than local leaders.

Although the implementation of the projects needs to be country-specific, the author suggests that regional or broader inter-country initiatives might be useful in raising awareness and strengthening capacity. Good practices from elsewhere have and should be used to inspire initiatives in other countries. However, this should mean the application of the idea and objectives rather than simply seeking to replicate the format or approach. In order for those involved in GRB initiatives to learn from each other, it is important for them to highlight and share experiences, both the strengths and weaknesses. No country can claim that its budget is totally gender responsive. Moreover, the success of the initiatives should not be measured only in terms of changes in budgets. Budlender points out that it is an objective in itself to get people – and especially women – involved and doing things. Similarly, building partnerships and changing the outlook of civil servants and other people in positions of power on gender issues may not be immediately visible in budget and policy terms, but can facilitate later changes.

The country profiles in section four make apparent the strengths and weaknesses, opportunities and challenges facing gender responsive budgets. In these, Budlender draws on her wide experience to offer an honest assessment of the projects and show both the successes and the failures.

Abbreviations

AFB	Alternative Federal Budget
AUPWAE	Association of Uganda Professional Women in Agriculture and Environment
AusAID	Australian Agency for International Development
Bank	World Bank
Centre	Collaborative Centre for Gender and Development
CEDAW	Convention on the Elimination of All Forms of Discrimination Against Women
CIDA	Canadian International Development Agency
CTFC	Commonwealth Fund for Technical Assistance
DANIDA	Danish Agency for Development Assistance
DAWN	Development Alternatives with Women for a New Era
DFID	Department for International Development
EEO	Equal Employment Opportunities
FemAct	Feminist Activism Coalition
FIDA	International Federation of Women Lawyers
FOWODE	Forum for Women in Democracy
GAD	Gender and Development
GERA	Gender and Economic Reform in Africa
GNP	Gross National Product
GMS	Gender Management System
Group	Women's Budget Group.
GTZ	Deutsche Gesellschaft für Technische Zusammenarbeit (German Technical Cooperation Agency)
HIPC	Highly Indebted Poor Countries
IBP	International Budget Project
IDRC	International Development Research Centre
IMF	International Monetary Fund
IPU	Inter-Parliamentary Union

KWIRC	Karnataka Women's Information and Resource Centre
LGU	Local Government Unit
MTEF	Medium-Term Expenditure Framework
MP	Member of Parliament
NACSW	National Action Committee on the Status of Women
NCRFW	National Council on the Role of Filipino Women
NGO	Non-governmental organisation
NOVIB	Netherlands Organisation for International Development Cooperation
PDPW	Philippine Development Plan for Women
PER	Public Expenditure Review
PIP	Public Investment Programme
PRSP	Poverty Reduction Strategy Paper
SAM	Social Accounting Matrix
SIDA	Swedish International Development Cooperation Agency
SWC	Status of Women Canada
TGNP	Tanzania Gender Networking Programme
UN	United Nations
UNDP	United Nations Development Programme
UNIFEM	United Nations Development Fund for Women
US AID	United States Agency for International Development
WBI	Women's Budget Initiative
WID	Women in Development
WIDE	Women in Development Europe

Integrating Gender into Government Budgets within a Context of Economic Reform*

Diane Elson

Introduction

Over the past decade there has been a growing recognition of the importance of macroeconomic policy in shaping women's living standards and their prospects for economic empowerment. It can worsen or improve the living standards of different groups of women and contribute to narrowing or widening gender gaps in incomes, health, education, nutrition, etc. The Commonwealth, in its work on women and structural adjustment, pioneered this recognition of and investigation into the implications of macroeconomic policy for women (Commonwealth Secretariat, 1989).

There has also been growing understanding of the way in which gender inequality can constrain the outcomes of macro-economic policy. For example, economic reforms with decreased incentives can reduce women's output, or restricted access to education or training can hamper women's ability to develop their human resources (Haddad *et al.*, 1995; Cagatay, Elson and Grown (eds), 1995; World Bank, 1995; Palmer, 1995).

One of the most important areas of macroeconomic policy is the national budget. The following section provides a rationale for gender responsive budgets. It then offers a wide range of analytical tools for the integration of a gender perspective into national budgets, with an emphasis on public expenditure. These tools should be applied according to national circumstances.

*Adapted from a paper presented to the Fifth Meeting of Commonwealth Ministers Responsible for Women's Affairs, Port of Spain, Trinidad and Tobago, November 1996.

The Economic Costs of Gender Inequality

There is growing awareness that gender inequality is inefficient; it is not only costly to women, but it is also costly to children and to many men. It exacts costs through lower output, reduced development of people's capacities, less leisure and diminished well-being. Women's economic empowerment would provide the possibility for all countries to have some combination of increased productivity, improved human resources, less stress and better overall health.

1. Research on agricultural productivity in Africa shows that reducing gender inequality could significantly increase agricultural yields. For instance, giving women farmers in Kenya the same level of agricultural inputs (seeds, fertilisers, pesticides, etc.) and education as men farmers could increase yields obtained by women farmers by more than 20 per cent (Saito and Spurling, 1992).

2. Research on economic growth and education shows that failing to invest in female education lowers the gross national product (GNP). Everything else being equal, countries in which the ratio of female-to-male enrolment in primary or secondary education is less than 0.75 can expect levels of GNP that are roughly 25 per cent lower than countries in which there is less gender disparity in education (Hill and King, 1995).

3. Research on gender inequality in the labour market shows that eliminating gender discrimination across occupations and in salaries and benefits could increase not only women's income but also national income. For example, if gender inequality in the labour market in Latin America were to be eliminated, not only could women's wages rise by about 50 per cent, but national output could rise by 5 per cent (Tzannatos, 1991).

4. Gender inequality also reduces the productivity of the next generation, while the World Bank reports mounting evidence that increases in women's well-being yield productivity gains in the future. The probability of children being enrolled in school increases with their mother's educational level, and extra income going to mothers has a

more positive impact on household investment in nutrition, health and education of children than extra income going to fathers (World Bank, 1995).

5. Research shows that gender inequality hampers a positive supply response to structural adjustment measures. When crop prices rise, economists expect farmers to produce more. But if the payments go mainly into the hands of male farmers, women farmers will not have a direct incentive to produce more. Even if some of the money does find its way to women farmers, they may not have time to produce more for the market because they are already at full stretch producing for their families, collecting water and fuel and looking after their children (Brown, 1995).

Women's time burdens are an important constraint on growth and development – women are an over-utilised, not an under-utilised resource. The benefits of reducing this gender-based constraint can be considerable. For instance, a study in Tanzania shows that reducing such constraints in a community of smallholder coffee and banana growers increases household cash incomes by 10 per cent, labour productivity by 15 per cent and capital productivity by 44 per cent (Tibaijuka, 1994).

It is important to be clear that recognising gender inequality as an efficiency issue does not mean seeing women instrumentally as a resource to be used by others for increasing productivity and growth. Rather the message is that if women themselves have more control over resources there will be gains for society as a whole; but if gender inequality persists, there will be continuing losses for society as a whole.

The Economic Gains from Gender Responsiveness

Macroeconomic policy can increase, reduce or leave unchanged the losses to society from gender inequality. This could occur through direct efforts and indirect effects. The examples from the previous section will be used to show how this might happen, through actions that alleviate or exacerbate gender inequality.

Productivity of women farmers in Africa. Macroeconomic policy could increase productivity by promoting a higher level of agricultural inputs and education for women or reduce it by lowering levels of inputs and education for women. An increase could occur through direct efforts, for example, by increasing public expenditure on schooling, extension services and credit (and possibly input subsidies) to women. An increase could also occur through indirect effects, for example, if macroeconomic policies promoted increases in family income which lead to families educating daughters to the same extent as sons; or promoted the increased provision of physical infrastructure (like water, sanitation, electricity) which releases more of adult women's time from domestic responsibilities to learn how to use new inputs. However, macroeconomic policy could also result in a lower level of education and inputs for women farmers. This might come directly from reductions in public expenditure on education and restrictions on credit and the abolition of subsidies. It might also come indirectly through policy-induced falls in family income which reduce the ability and willingness to educate daughters; or by promoting reduced provision of physical infrastructure, thereby increasing women's total time burdens so that they are less able to spend time learning how to use new inputs.

Gender disparities in education. Macroeconomic policy can increase losses in potential GNP if it increases gender gaps in education. This can happen directly through reduced expenditure on education, and indirectly through increases in family poverty. However, losses can be reduced if macroeconomic policies promote increases in expenditure on education, especially at the primary level, and at the same time reduce family poverty so that families can afford to send daughters to school.

Labour market inequalities. Macroeconomic policy can reduce labour market inequality directly by extending public sector employment for women, since gender inequality in employment in the public sector is generally less than in the private sector, or by removing differentials in salaries, conditions or employment opportunities between men and women through employment policies. It can reduce labour market inequality indirectly by promoting forms of economic growth that create new jobs for women, such as an expansion of the garment or electronics industry. However, care has to be taken that inequalities in total workload – paid and unpaid – are not at the same time increased.

The supply response to structural adjustment measures. Macroeconomic policy can intensify rather than alleviate the ways in which gender inequality constrains women's ability to increase production in response to structural adjustment measures. Gender inequality can constrain the supply response (changes in output) if women have many other demands on their time – producing food, fetching water and fuel, caring for children – and if they have the prime responsibility for cushioning their families against insecurity and change. These constraints would be intensified directly if macroeconomic policies reduce the provision of social and infrastructural services that cause an increase in women's time-burdens. They would be intensified indirectly if macroeconomic policies increase the insecurity and change to which families are subject.

These examples demonstrate the importance of analysing whether macroeconomic policy increases or reduces the costs to society from gender inequality. There are clear gains if macroeconomic policy can be designed in ways that reduce or eliminate gender inequality. The gains to society from the reduction of gender inequality can be a combination of impacts, which include:

- increased output of goods and services;
- increased leisure;
- increased capability to live a satisfying life (such as the enjoyment of good health, exercise of skills and participation in decision making);
- increased conservation of the environment.

Macroeconomic Policy and the National Budget

Macroeconomics looks at an economy as a series of aggregates of goods and services: the GNP, exports, imports, savings, investment, public expenditure on services and income transfers, and public revenue (from taxes and user charges).

Macroeconomic policy generally attempts to steer the economy as a whole towards achieving sustainable improvements in national output and incomes (e.g. full employment, rising incomes, stable prices). However, improvements will not be sustainable if they are based on unmanageable deficits in the balance of payments and in the national budget (which brings together public expenditure and public revenue). So a great deal of attention is focused on these twin deficits, as well as on the rate of inflation, the rate of unemployment and the rate of growth.

There is a tendency to assume that there is no need for macroeconomic policy to pay explicit attention to human development objectives. Problems of poverty and inequality would be resolved by 'trickle down' of benefits from the macroeconomic aggregates (and national economic prosperity). However, there is growing recognition that 'trickle down' is not automatic; rather, concerns of poverty and inequality, including gender inequality, need to be brought directly into the framework of macroeconomic policy.

There are three key forms of macroeconomic policy:

- exchange rate policy (e.g. currency appreciation and depreciation);
- monetary policy (e.g. money supply and interest rates); and
- fiscal policy (e.g. taxation and public expenditure).

These three types of policy are used in combination in stabilisation and structural adjustment programmes and in restructuring economies to meet the challenges of changing international patterns of investment and production.

Fiscal policy is considered to be the most promising entry point for integrating a gender analysis. There are a variety of instruments of fiscal policy, which can be grouped under revenue or expenditure:

Revenue instruments: Taxes: e.g. income tax, expenditure tax (e.g. value added tax, or VAT), wealth tax, land tax, tariffs on imports, capital gains tax, inheritance tax. User charges: e.g. for electricity, water, education, health.

Expenditure instruments: Transfers: e.g. pensions, unemployment benefits, maternity benefits. Subsidies: e.g. food subsidies, export subsidies. Services: e.g. law and order, health, education, roads.

Typically these are all brought together in a national budget, which is prepared annually and sets out tax and expenditure plans for the coming year. If expenditure is greater than revenue there is a deficit; if revenue is greater than expenditure, a surplus. The budget is often accompanied by a review of budget outcomes and macroeconomic performance in the previous year and, in a 'medium-term expenditure framework', projections of budget outcomes and macroeconomic performance for future years. For countries undergoing stabilisation or structural adjustment programmes, the medium-term expenditure framework will be related to a policy framework paper.

The budget, on the face of it, appears to be a gender-neutral policy instrument. It is set out in terms of financial aggregates: totals and sub-totals of expenditure and revenue, and the resulting budget surplus or deficit. There is no particular mention of women, nor a particular mention of men either. However, this appearance of gender neutrality is more accurately described as 'gender blindness', since the national budget generally ignores the different socially determined roles, responsibilities and capabilities of men and women, and usually overlooks the different impacts that policies have on men and women in the country.

Gender blindness exists in the conceptual frameworks and statistics used to prepare national budgets (see Waring, 1989; Cagatay, Elson and Grown (eds), 1995). They fail to recognise that:

1. Women's contribution to the macroeconomy is underestimated because of biased markets and missing and incomplete statistics;

2. There is an unpaid economy (which has been variously labelled 'domestic', 'social reproduction', 'reproductive') in which women do most of the work of caring for and maintaining the labour force and the social framework or social capital (neighbourhood networks and voluntary

organisations, formal and informal), which are vital services for the paid economy; and,

3. The parameters of aggregate production, savings, investment, imports and exports in the paid economy may be sensitive to different patterns of gender relations and gender distribution of resources.

Integrating Gender into the National Budget: Applying Analytical Tools

Formulation of a national budget involves decisions at three levels:

- ***Aggregate macroeconomic strategy.*** Is the overall deficit or surplus appropriate? Is the medium-term economic policy framework sustainable?
- ***Composition of expenditures and revenues.*** Is the mix of spending and taxing appropriate?
- ***Effectiveness of service delivery.*** Does the public sector provide the required level and pattern of services to firms, families and communities?

A range of tools for integrating gender into these three levels of decision-making is available. They can be used individually or in combination, depending upon the circumstances of the country. The most readily implementable options relate to efficiency of service delivery and composition of expenditures, but some tools are also available in relation to taxation and aggregate macroeconomic strategy. A comprehensive strategy could use the full range of tools to produce a gender responsive budget (GRB) statement and a gender-aware medium-term economic policy framework, possibly supported by a gender management system (GMS). But more partial strategies can also bring about considerable improvements. Six tools that have proved particularly useful are listed in Annex 1 with examples of their use.

The tools addressed below are mainly concerned with public expenditure, as commissioned by the Commonwealth Secretariat for this programme. It would be appropriate to have a follow-up component which addresses revenue raising measures – transfer payments, taxes and user charges; and to encourage the implementation of this programme in developed countries as well as in developing countries.

Integrating Gender into the Appraisal of the Effectiveness of Service Delivery

The effectiveness of public expenditure is conventionally judged in terms of the achievement of intended results at the lowest possible cost. From a gender perspective, it is important to ask: 'results for whom?' and 'costs to whom?'. Do the outcomes meet the needs of women as well as men? Are men and women equally satisfied with the quality of services provided? Is the quality assessed in ways that take account of the needs of users for 'user-friendly services'? Are the costs and benefits measured in a comprehensive way? Do the intended results include reduction of gender inequality? A range of techniques are available or might be developed for addressing these questions:

- needs assessments;
- analysis of 'quality of service' indicators;
- beneficiary assessments;
- assessments of 'invisible' costs; and
- assessments of benefits of equal opportunities in service delivery.

Needs assessments: Needs assessments attempt to establish what services are required and where, and are typically carried out by gathering quantitative data on the demographic characteristics, income levels and services available in localities throughout the country and combining these into poverty indicators of various kinds. The problem is that the data is often not disaggregated by gender, and the needs are not defined from the point of view of the users of services. Moreover, the need for time is not generally considered and time-poverty is neglected. However, a useful point of departure is provided by some of the more participatory and gender-aware World Bank Poverty Assessments (e.g. World Bank, 1994), and by a variety of case studies conducted by Women's Studies Institutes and women's organisations, using participatory appraisal methods.

Analysis of quality service indicators: An analysis of 'quality of service' is done through constructing a series of quantitative indicators (enrolment rates in schools, bed occupancy rates in hospitals, number of connections of households to water and sanitation systems). However, there are well known problems. One is that it is easier to measure inputs than outputs. All of the above measures are actually input measures, but we really need to know how many students passed their exams, how many patients were cured and how many households had reliable supplies of clean drinking water. In addition, the indicators may not measure the qualities that matter most to users of the services. It is obviously essential to make sure the indicators are disaggregated by gender.

Beneficiary assessments: A beneficiary assessment tries to ascertain the views of actual and potential beneficiaries, to see how far service provisions meet their own perceptions of what their needs are. Beneficiary assessments are best conducted using qualitative interviewing or focus group methods. Care must be taken to conduct them in ways that permit and encourage women to express their views. It is particularly important to assess whether measures that are supposed to improve effectiveness actually do improve the quality of service from a beneficiary's perspective.

Assessment of 'invisible' costs: From a gender perspective it is important to define costs so as to include costs in terms of time as well as money. Many current changes in the organisation of service delivery appear to improve efficiency but in reality transfer costs from the monetary budgets of the public sector, where they are visible, to the time budgets of women in families and communities, where they are generally invisible. Every proposal to improve the efficiency of a service should be scrutinised for the real extent of its 'cost saving' measures. For example, when medical services are reorganised so as to save costs by discharging patients more rapidly from hospitals, does this simply transfer costs of care from paid hospital staff to unpaid women in families and communities? If so, this is not a saving in costs, but a transfer of costs.

Assessment of benefits of equal opportunities in service delivery: Public sector employment policies can help to transform gender relations throughout the economy by offering innovative equal opportunities and family-friendly employment practices. A gender-blind cost benefit calculus may see these policies as 'too expensive'. A gender-sensitive cost-benefit calculus will see that such policies set standards and promote better practices throughout the economy, reducing the extent of gender discrimination in labour markets and enhancing women's ability to invest in the human resource development of themselves and their children, with resulting efficiency gains.

Public sector procurement policies can also help offset existing gender disadvantage, producing benefits that ripple through the larger economy. Procurement policies in some countries (such as South Africa) are already linked to equal opportunities policies directed at reducing disadvantages of race as well as gender. Measures include:

- simplifying the tender process;
- easier access to tender information; and
- unbundling of large contracts.

To reduce inequality, consideration may also be given to the use of short-term 'price preferences' and quota or target systems biased in favour of women-owned businesses. Such businesses may be allowed to win a contract at a price which is a little above the lowest bid from a business owned by a man.

Integrating Gender into Appraisal of the Composition of Public Expenditure

Different patterns of expenditure and taxation have different implications for women and men and differentially affect their abilities to contribute to production for the market and the care of families and communities. In the language of economics, these different patterns 'crowd-in' or 'crowd-out' supply responses of men and women to macroeconomic strategies.

Rhonda Sharp (1990), an economist and policy analyst who has worked extensively on the integration of a gender analysis into the Federal and State Budgets in Australia, suggests a conceptual framework for reporting the expenditure of each government department within three categories of expenditure: expenditure specifically targeted at women; equal opportunity initiatives in the public sector; and gender impact of mainstream budget expenditure. Pictorially she presents it this way:

TOTAL BUDGET EXPENDITURE

=

Specifically identified gender-based expenditures of government departments and authorities

- Women's health programmes;
- Special education initiatives for girls;
- Employment policy initiatives for women;

and so on

+

Equal employment opportunity expenditure by government departments and authorities on their employees

- Training for clerical officers or women managers;
- Rewriting job descriptions to reflect equal employment opportunity principles;
- Provision of crèche facilities;
- Parental leave provisions;

and so on

+

General or mainstream budget expenditure by government departments and authorities assessed for its gender impact

Does the education budget, minus the above two types of expenditure, reflect gender equity objectives?

Who are the users of hospital services?

Who receives agricultural support services?

Decisions about the allocation of expenditure to different uses are generally made without considering the gender distribution of benefits and costs. A number of tools are available which help to fill this gap and to throw light on the gender implications of 'general or mainstream' expenditure. These are:

- public expenditure incidence analysis;
- budgetary institutions;
- gender-aware policy appraisal; and
- women's or gender budget statement.

Public expenditure incidence analysis: A useful tool for helping to assess the distribution of public spending by gender is public expenditure incidence analysis (or benefit incidence analysis). It can provide one way of assessing how gender-inclusive such expenditure actually is by comparing the distribution of spending between men and women, boys and girls.

The first step is to analyse the net unit costs of providing any service, i.e. the annual total costs of public provision of the service minus the proceeds of any cost recovery measures (e.g. user charges). This total is then divided by the annual number of 'units' of the service provided (e.g. the number of hospital beds or school places). The second step is to analyse the pattern of utilisation of the services, for instance, how many 'units' were utilised by poor households and how many by rich households.

The information on net unit costs of service provision can be brought together with the information on utilisation rates to calculate the level of net resource transfer to poor households and to rich households. This statistic is called the 'incidence of public expenditure by income group'. In principle, this procedure could be extended to measure the incidence of public expenditure by gender, by examining the pattern of utilisation of services by gender, as well as by household income grouping. This has been done for health and education in Ghana (Demetry *et al.*, 1995).

Data, collected from the relevant public service providers, is required on the amount spent at national, regional and local level on provision of a particular service. This is often surprisingly difficult to assemble and decentralisation of expenditure to lower tiers of government tends to make it even harder. The contracting out of public services may also create data problems. Definition of an appropriate unit of service is relatively easy for some services, such as health (e.g. visits to doctor) and education (attendance at school), but very difficult in the case of 'overhead' type services, such as most physical infrastructure. Data is also required on utilisation rates from regular national household surveys. Unfortunately, not all household surveys collected data on utilisation of public services and the data may not be collected on a gender-disaggregated basis. Thus, it may be necessary to improve the available database in collaboration with the Ministry of Finance, the National Audit Commission (or similar body) and the Office of Statistics.

Budgetary institutions: Budgetary institutions play an important role in the determination of patterns of public expenditure and taxation, and economic reform increasingly includes reform of budget processes, with an emphasis on improving accountability and transparency. It is therefore important to appraise the institutional gender-balance in budgetary decision-making and the interface between the Gender Management System and the Budget or Financial Management System. Here, an important tool is an analysis of the share of the total budget which goes to the Ministry Responsible for Women's Affairs compared to other Ministries and, within each ministry/department, the share of its budget controlled by its gender focal point (or comparable unit). Gender cannot be 'mainstreamed' if those who have responsibility for mainstreaming gender are not given budget allocations for this goal.

Gender-aware policy appraisal: Gender-disaggregated incidence analysis is not readily applicable to some forms of expenditure, because the services provided are not individually but collectively consumed. For example, much of the expenditure of the Ministry of Trade and Industry or Transport or Power will be difficult to subject to gender-disaggregated benefit incidence analysis. But the types of facilities provided and policies pursued by these Ministries can be appraised from a gender perspective. Here gender-aware policy appraisal can be used instead. The key question is whether the policies are likely to reduce gender inequalities and imbalances. The Women's Budget Project in South Africa, a joint initiative of the Parliamentary Finance Committee and NGOs, provides a good example (see country profile).

Women's or gender budget statement: A women's budget statement can be an important tool for bringing together information on the implications of government expenditures for women. Such a statement does not produce a separate budget for women. Rather it attempts to disaggregate expenditure according to its impact on women. As pioneered in Australia, participating government departments were required to identify how their proposed expenditure would affect women. A women's budget statement was then synthesised by the Office of the Status of Women. The production of a women's budget statement thus requires a high degree of co-operation and some degree of commitment throughout the machinery of government. The creation of the conditions for this probably requires a substantial and well-organised coalition of supporters both inside and outside of government. A number of strengths and weaknesses of the system used in Australia, have been identified by Australian policy analysts (Sharp, 1990; Sawyer, 1996) (see below).

The effectiveness of a women's budget statement could be improved by making use of some of the analysis and indicators suggested here. Indeed some of these measures have already been introduced in parts of Australia. For instance, for the 1989/90 South Australian women's budget, departments were asked to provide their own internal indicators of progressive changes and to detail the expected future outcomes of current expenditures. However, tackling the issue of overall budgetary strategy requires going beyond a women's budget statement.

Integration of a Gender Appraisal of the Overall Macroeconomic Strategy and Medium-Term Economic Policy Framework

The appraisal of an aggregate budgetary strategy depends on a judgement about how far the budget deficit or surplus is sustainable in the future. This is conventionally judged in terms

Strengths	Weaknesses
Awareness-raising: educational role in sensitising ministries/departments to the implications of their policies for women, and helping them to reduce their 'gender-blindness'.	Inability to effectively analyse the impact of 'mainstream' expenditure on women – no guidelines were provided for Departments on how to do this.
Capacity building: lever for the production of gender-specific data.	Inability to address issues of overall design of budgetary policy – e.g. how much should expenditure be cut; which expenditure should be cut.
Advocacy: useful resource for women in government for entering into debates about specific budgetary policies.	Ignores revenue side of budget and interactions between budget expenditure in different Ministries for overall situation of women.
	Does not provide quantifiable measures of improvements over time.

of whether a deficit will tend to lead to financial problems, such as accelerating inflation, balance of payments crises or an increasing and unsustainable debt burden. Although a budget surplus that tends not to lead to financial problems is not always judged to be a problem, a deficit that is too low or a surplus that is too high may lead to unemployment, poverty and low levels of capacity utilisation. This overburdens families and communities, with consequent social and economic problems, and intensifies losses due to gender inequality.

The likely sustainability of a budget deficit is often tested by using a computable macroeconomic model to simulate the likely outcomes with a range of different values for variables. But the answers will depend on the assumption built into the model. Negative feedback from overburdening families and communities is not built into such models, nor is negative feedback due to the efficiency costs of worsening gender inequalities.

One of the factors that is usually assumed to be constant is the social framework of norms, rules and values (what some economists call the 'social capital'). For instance, to work well an economy needs a fund of goodwill, trust and acceptance of and obedience to the law. There should also be some institutions that provide social stability and security, even though the economy is changing, and that can cushion individuals against shocks and see them through times of transition and restructuring. However, the social framework may need not to be at odds with the macroeconomic policy. High and rising deficits that generate hyperinflation will tend to lead the social framework to crumble, but so also will severely deflationary policies in which the deficit is cut rapidly and extensively, creating widespread unemployment and idle capacity. Some economists are now beginning to pay attention to the interrelation between macroeconomic polices and the social framework. They are asking whether in some circumstances too rapid a deflation, as well as too rapid an inflation, runs down to dangerous levels the fund of goodwill and acceptance of social norms that is needed for economies to function well and for the stability of the wider operating environment.

A critical factor in the maintenance of the social framework is the unpaid work that women in particular devote to bringing up children to be responsible members of society, and in strengthening family and community networks and voluntary organisations. Central to the destruction of the social framework is the amount of idle time that young men have because they are denied paid work.

Two tools that are useful for examining feedbacks between macroeconomic variables and gender relations are:

- gender-disaggregated analysis of the impact of the budget on time use; and
- gender-aware medium-term economic policy frameworks.

Gender-disaggregated analysis of the impact of the budget on time use: A GRB strategy can be promoted by monitoring the time budgets of a country's citizens as well as the financial budget of the country. This information may be available from regular household surveys. If not, then time use questions, disaggregated by gender and age, will need to be added. In the short run, useful data may be gathered by women's organisations using rapid appraisal techniques at selected sites. Such techniques include holding focus group discussions or asking members to keep a diary of what they did the day before.

Armed with time budgets, it is possible to frame another question to set alongside the question of the sustainability of the deficit in the national budget. This is: 'Is the deficit in women's time budget between the demands of unpaid work, and the time left available for it, sustainable or are the human resources of women or girls being depleted?'

If the time deficit becomes too high, there will be negative feedback effects to the market economy which reduce productivity and increase costs, very often leading to the need to increase public expenditure to repair damage to the social framework. This could include, for instance, expenditure on insurance, policing, social workers or repairs to public property. Ultimately this undermines the sustainability of the budget strategy.

Thus, if the budget deficit has been reduced by expenditure cutbacks that place great reliance on women's reproductive and voluntary work to substitute for public services, while at the same time making men surplus to requirements, then there is a danger that its sustainability will prove illusory in the long run. Certainly, budget policy will not be providing a good foundation for the longer run achievement of growth combined with human development, because it is depleting human and social resources. The same interactions might also occur if budget policy leads to high and accelerating inflation, which can also put too much strain on the time budget of the care economy, using up large amounts of time in reorganising household management in the face of corrosive uncertainties about prices.

The critical point is that a gender responsive approach to the overall budget strategy suggests that the maintenance of the social framework should not be taken for granted in judging the sustainability of budgets. Collecting time budget data is one way of making the connection. If time budgets look unsustainable, then this points to some reconsideration of the size of the national budget deficit, the tax-expenditure mix and the composition of expenditure

Gender-aware medium-term economic policy frameworks: Depending on the nature of the model used to simulate budget outcomes, some of the parameters may well be sensitive to the gendered nature of control over resources or the distribution of resources between women and men. For instance, the evidence on gender equality as an efficiency issue suggests that the productivity of investment could be raised by changing the gender distribution of resources in favour of women. Moreover, if women have a greater propensity to save than men, redistributing income towards women would raise the aggregate savings rate. Exploring this possibility requires some technical knowledge of modelling and cooperation with the economists in the Ministry of Finance who work with the models in use in a particular country.

A complementary strategy would be to examine the gender responsiveness of the institutional orientation or social system in which the overall budget strategy is embedded. If women have more voice in the social bargaining that, implicitly or explicitly, impacts on macroeconomic policy-making then more cooperative, less inflationary responses to any given deficit may result. For instance, owing to differences in their roles, women may have a different view than men of the trade-off between wage increases and maintenance or improvement of public sector services that support their caring roles. Women may be more prepared than men to accept limited wage increases in return for maintenance of public expenditure. A greater consideration of women's point of view should, other things being equal, lessen the risk of an inflationary spiral. This is not something that can be brought about quickly, but it should be possible to create opportunities for women to express their priorities through instruments such as attitude surveys, focus groups, public meetings and the media. This needs to be matched by an increase in the representation of women in parliament and in the executive, political and civil service, especially those determining budget policy. The outcome could be a number of different budget scenarios, depending on the gender distribution of resources and the level of empowerment of women.

The relevance of this last point is that the possibility of budget policy that is 'sound', promoting a human-centred pattern of growth, depends not only on seemingly mechanical economic factors, but also on social and political factors. Successful budget policy does require certain technical skills, and is constrained by available resources, but it is also an exercise in political economy, social bargaining and coalition building and in creating informed consent ('social contracts' or 'social compacts') around a shared vision of development. An alternative GRB and medium-term economic policy framework may be a powerful focus for such a vision.

Taking Action

Decisions on budget policy are usually taken by a small group of Ministers and officials in the Head of Government's Office, Ministry of Finance and/or Central Bank. Ministers and officials in Ministries Responsible for Women's Affairs, who are outside this group, need to engage in policy dialogue with the budget officials to promote the use of the tools identified here to bring about changes in budget policy so as to reduce gender inequality. Policy dialogue needs to be broadened through a multi-pronged strategy to incorporate the perspectives of different actors and interest groups, which could include:

- ministries/departments which are responsible for major expenditure, such as health, education and agriculture;
- parliamentarians, lawmakers and women's political caucuses;
- women's organisations, NGOs and development agencies;
- researchers, academics and policy analysts; and
- the general public.

The aim would be to stimulate demand for integrating a gender analysis into fiscal policy and the budget cycle. Ministers Responsible for Women's Affairs have a crucial role in increasing the understanding of 'why' and 'how' budgets can be made gender responsive, by:

1. Initiating a process of collaboration among officials from the Ministry Responsible for Women's Affairs,

the Ministry of Finance and the key spending ministries, together with the relevant civil society groups, to integrate a gender analysis into government budgets.

2. Promoting the development and use of gender-sensitive macroeconomic concepts and models in the design of budget policy, with the aim of producing a number of different GRB scenarios.

3. Supporting 'budget hearings' among women parliamentarians and women's organisations in order for them to voice their opinion on the gender impacts of government budgets.

The Commonwealth Secretariat has already taken measures to facilitate a policy dialogue by including gender and macroeconomic policy issues on the agenda of the meetings of Commonwealth Finance Ministers and Ministers Responsible for Women's Affairs.

Conclusion

The integration of a gender perspective into budgetary policy has both equality and efficiency dimensions, thereby contributing to more effective policy design. A gender responsive budget would create a virtuous circle in which the policy itself contributes to the reduction of gender inequality, and hence lessens gender constraints to successful macroeconomic outcomes. The result is the simultaneous improvement of economic growth and human development performance in ways that also empower women.

Annex: Gender Responsive Budget Analytical Tools[1]

The tools listed below, with examples of country application, are used for carrying out GRB analysis:

Tool 1: Gender-Aware Policy Appraisal is the analysis from a gender perspective of the policies and programmes funded through the budget, which asks 'in what ways are the policies and their associated resource allocations likely to reduce or increase gender inequality?'

Example: *The South African government's land reform programme is proceeding at an increasing pace, with corresponding increases in expenditure for everything from owner compensation to micro-finance programmes. However, women's access to land as well as to the financial resources necessary for its development is impeded by legal restrictions on women's land ownership and rights to conclude contracts. Women who do have access to land tend to have access to smaller plots with poor irrigation, and women-headed households typically have no wage or salary earners. As a result, women are far less able to benefit from the reform process and related expenditures. The Department of Land Affairs has started to integrate gender concerns into its monitoring and evaluation system and has begun providing gender training for staff.*

Tool 2: Beneficiary Assessments. Beneficiary assessment is a means by which the voice of the citizen can be heard. In these exercises, the actual or potential beneficiaries of public services are asked to assess how far public spending is meeting their needs, as they perceive them. This can be done through opinion polls, attitude surveys, group discussion or interviews. Questions focus on overall priorities for public spending or on the details of the operation of public services.

Example: *In the United States, alarm over a national debt 'crisis' reached a peak in the mid-1990s, creating pressure to cut government expenditures in order to reduce the deficit. In 1996, the Women's International League for Peace and Freedom initiated a Women's Budget Project, asking women to answer a series of questions about*

1 Adapted from Elson, 2000b.

the choices they would make in allocating national budget resources. Pointing out that few women benefit from military spending programmes because they are severely under-represented both in the armed forces and in military contractor jobs, the project calculated the costs of various defence-related programmes and compared them to potential social welfare expenditures. It then asked: Which would you choose? Fund the F-22 fighter plane programme for the current year ($2.1 billion) or pay for the annual health care expenses for 1.3 million American women? Fund 'Sea wolf' attack submarines for the current year ($1.7 billion) or provide low-income home energy assistance for 5.6 million households? The project estimated the savings from proposed cuts in military spending and outlined the ways in which such savings could be invested to benefit women, including employment and training programmes, campaigns against gender-based violence and services for the elderly, the majority of whom are women.

Tool 3: Gender-disaggregated Public Expenditure Incidence Analysis estimates the distribution of budget resources (or changes in resources) among males and females by measuring the unit costs of providing a given service and multiplying that cost by the number of units used by each group. Incidence analysis of public expenditure is a useful tool for helping to assess the gender distribution of public spending. It can give a sense of how gender-inclusive such expenditures actually are by comparing the distribution of the benefits of public spending among women and men, girls and boys. Similarly it can suggest the gender impact of supposedly gender-neutral budget cuts.

Example: *Changes to Sri Lanka's food ration and subsidy programme in the 1980s revealed that, despite rapid economic growth, the real value of food stamps eroded in the first half of the decade and there was a decline in the real incomes of the poor. A gender-disaggregated analysis concluded that within poor households, girls and women took the brunt of the increasing food deficit, citing higher levels of malnutrition among pre-school and school-aged girls and declining birth weights of babies born to low income mothers.*

Tool 4: Gender-Disaggregated Analysis of the Impact of the Budget on Time Use is a calculation of the link between budget allocations and their effect on how household members spend their time, using household time use surveys. Changes in government resource allocation have impacts on the way in which time is spent in households. In particular, cuts in some forms of public expenditure are likely to increase the amount of time that women have to spend in unpaid care work for their families and communities in order to make up for lost public services. Thus whenever cuts are proposed, the question should be asked: 'Is this likely to increase the time that men and women spend on unpaid care provision?'

Example: *Between 1983 and 1985, real per-capita expenditure on health fell by 16 per cent in Zambia. People had to travel greater distances and wait for longer period of time to get treatment and drugs. Interviewed Zambian women reported having to spend more time caring for sick family members, including time spent with them in hospital providing meals and helping to nurse them.*

Tool 5: Gender-Aware Medium-Term Economic Policy Framework is used to assess the impact of economic policies on women, focusing on aggregate fiscal, monetary and economic policies designed to promote globalisation and reduce poverty. The ultimate aim of gender analyses of government budgets is to incorporate gender variables into the models on which medium-term public expenditure planning are based. This can be done by disaggregating, by sex, variables that refer to people (e.g., labour supply) or including new variables to represent the unpaid care economy.

Example: *In South Africa the government invited members of the Women's Budget Initiative to address a workshop on the development of the 1996 Medium Term Expenditure Framework (MTEF). The idea was to plan expenditure on a three-year rolling basis rather than on the present year-by-year rolling basis. It is noteworthy that while this did not mean that the MTEF would necessarily be gender-sensitive, it did signal a willingness by the Ministry of Finance to engage with gender-equality issues. In fact, the National Expenditure Survey produced by the Ministry of Finance in 1999 did incorporate more gender analysis. In Tanzania, the Ministry of Finance is seeking to integrate gender concerns into the new MTEF and performance budgeting system.*

Tool 6: Gender Responsive Budget Statement is the government report that reviews the budget using some of the above tools, and summarises its implications for gender equality with different indicators, such as the share of expenditure targeted to gender equality, the gender balance in government jobs, contracts or training, or the share of public service expenditure used mainly by women. Any government can issue a GRB statement utilising one or more of the above tools to analyse its programmes and budgets and summarise their implications with a number of key indicators. It requires a high degree of coordination throughout the public sector and is essentially an accountability report by government regarding its commitment to gender equity.

Example: *The Commonwealth Secretariat Gender Responsive Budget Initiative identified possible indicators that could be used to prepare a GRB statement. These indicators were proposed as starting points for a continuous process of monitoring resource allocations and linking these to government commitments and policies. They included:*

- *the share of total expenditure targeted to gender equality programmes;*
- *gender balance in public-sector employment, which looks at the number of women and men at different levels and in different jobs;*
- *the share of expenditure devoted to women's priority needs from public services;*
- *the share of expenditure devoted to the national women's machinery and to the gender units within each Ministry;*
- *the share of expenditure on income transfers devoted to women's priorities, which would include child-support grants that provide monthly payments to care-givers of young children in poor households;*
- *gender balance in business support, such as the subsidies, training or credit provided by the Ministries of Trade and Industry, and Agriculture;*
- *gender balance in public sector contracts awarded, including contracts to build houses or for public works;*
- *gender balance in membership of government committees and other decision-making bodies and fora; and*
- *gender balance in government training programmes.*

Promoting Gender Equality Through Public Expenditure*

Guy Hewitt and Tanni Mukhopadhyay

Introduction

The Commonwealth's impetus towards encouraging member countries to integrate gender concerns into economic policy dates back to the 1980s and the report of the Commonwealth Expert Group on Women and Structural Adjustment, *Engendering Adjustment for the 1990s* and the *Ottawa Declaration on Women and Structural Adjustment*, endorsed by Heads of Government in 1991. The Expert Group report called for the incorporation of gender concerns in the areas of public expenditure, taxation, credit policies, exchange rate policies, pricing policies, wage policies, trade liberalisation and privatisation. Gender equality has long been an objective asserted and affirmed by Commonwealth member countries and the Commonwealth Secretariat in various national, regional and international fora.

In the framework of the 1995 *Commonwealth Plan of Action on Gender and Development*, Commonwealth Finance Ministers at their meeting held in Malta in 2000 'reaffirmed the importance of the Commonwealth Secretariat's programme on gender equality'. They also welcomed the Commonwealth Gender Budget Initiative and 'looked forward to the review of the pilot stage of their project'. Such a review is undertaken in this section, which uses a gender analysis, implemented through gender responsive budget (GRB) initiatives, as a pivotal

*This paper was prepared for the September 2001 meeting of Commonwealth Finance Ministers. However, like many other international meetings due to be held that month, the meeting was cancelled following the tragic events in the USA.

We pledge the Commonwealth and our countries to work with renewed vigour, concentrating especially ... [on] equality for women, so that they may exercise their full and equal rights.

Harare Commonwealth Declaration, 1991

Under the Commonwealth Plan of Action governments agreed to the integration of gender issues in all national policies, plans and programmes; and to conduct gender policy appraisals of macroeconomic policies.

1995 Commonwealth Plan of Action on Gender and Development

Ministers of Finance [are] requested to endorse the integration of a gender analysis into the national budget.

Sixth Meeting of Commonwealth Ministers Responsible for Women's Affairs, New Delhi 2000

theme and tool with which to assess budgetary performance and impact.

The section outlines some of the issues that have been raised about making the design and management of public finances more gender responsive. It focuses on Commonwealth experiences of GRB work, drawing on those initiatives that have been undertaken at national, provincial and/or local levels and initiated or supported by the Commonwealth Secretariat programme or linked to it through processes of collaboration or information sharing. A conceptual framework for gender responsive budgets is also provided, supplying the rationale for public expenditure for gender equality within a wider context of promoting economic growth and supporting social inclusion and human resource development. Finally, based on these experiences, suggestions are made for strengthening GRB initiatives for implementation on a wider scale.

Background

States need to take primary responsibility for creating social infrastructure, which is largely beyond the capacity or interest of the private sector. Stiglitz (1996) argues that a vital role of all governments is to establish infrastructure in the broadest sense: *financial, physical, technological, educational, environmental* and *social*. Within these six areas of responsibility, Stiglitz suggests that the State in developing and transitional economies should take on further specific responsibilities due to the greater incidence of market failure in comparison with the developed world.

However, as the human, financial and institutional resources are often limited, particularly in developing and transitional economies, the formulation of development strategies needs to combine both the requirement for governmental intervention and the reality of the limitations to governmental action. This calls for balancing the strengths and limitations of markets and governments and determining how they best complement each other. Such a pragmatic approach needs to be adopted in the development of a framework for determining the specific requirements of countries and the role of governments in promoting socially responsive policies within their particular political and economic contexts.

Sound macroeconomic policy is undoubtedly a necessary basis for sustained and rapid economic growth. Central to this understanding is the recognition that social investments, such as the provision of basic healthcare, education and other essential services, can have prohibitively high social and economic costs if left to chance in the market place. There is also an increasing recognition that economic growth is a necessary but not sufficient condition for the reduction of poverty. Rather, the distribution of resources in a society has a crucial bearing on the manner in which growth impacts on poverty and, consequently, the development strategy pursued by governments in tackling inequalities is crucial (Watt, 2000).

State intervention in the market is therefore necessary to ensure that both efficiency and equity objectives are met. This recognises the fact that inequality not only slows growth but is also socially and politically costly. The reduction of poverty and promotion of social equity make good economic sense and are also considered to be moral imperatives. The recognition that distributional issues are central to eliminating poverty and inequality has prompted international organisations and countries to pursue developmental goals that redirect resources to poor and marginalised groups. Yet there remains a gap between declarations and commitments to these objectives and actual policy implementation. GRB initiatives are a useful tool to bridge this gap.

Public finance management is increasingly integrating developmental concerns, particularly those relating to social inclusion, human resource development and poverty eradication, within budgetary requirements of fiscal prudence, economic growth and political realism. This is undoubtedly a necessary but difficult task as hard choices have to be made in the face of competing demands, given the limited resources for financing various social priorities.

As the equity and distributional objectives have to be provided within the limited budgets and public funds available to governments, 'targeting' is the most cost-effective way of reaching those left behind or those most at risk. This means the concentration of resources towards meeting the needs of vulnerable groups within society. Undertaking gender responsive budgets helps to provide a more effective strategy for targeting, and a basis for the wider integration of gender analyses in macroeconomic planning.

What are Gender Responsive Budgets?[1]

Gender responsive budgets provide a means for determining the effect of government revenue and expenditure policies on women and men. GRB initiatives can consist of different components and vary considerably across countries and regions given their specific social, political contexts, and the nature of the institution implementing them. These initiatives, led either by governments or civil society groups, involve the examination

1 There are a variety of names for processes aimed at assessing the gender impacts of government budgets (see glossary).

of how budgetary allocations affect the economic and social opportunities of women and men. The exercise does not propose separate budgets for women nor necessarily argue for increased spending to women-specific programmes.

GRB initiatives seek to create a direct linkage between social and economic policies through the application of a gender analysis to the formulation and implementation of government budgets. Other categories, such as race and ethnicity, caste and class, age or geography could additionally disaggregate GRB initiatives. For instance, the South African 'women's budget' exercise combined a race analysis with its gender analysis in order to determine the impacts of government expenditure on white men and white women compared to their counterparts in other racial groups. However, because gender relations, that is, the power relations between and available opportunities for women and men, permeate all levels of economic, political, social and cultural life, gender analyses have been the primary focus. A gender analysis can also demonstrate the ways in which social institutions that are seemingly 'gender neutral' do in fact bear and transmit gender biases.

In Barbados, the exercise sought to incorporate and respond to notions of 'male under-performance' by examining correlations between expenditure and examination performance in the single sex schools. The research indicated higher performance at the girls' school compared to the boys' school, despite lower expenditure. However, the study was not designed to assess the impact of predominately female teachers in both schools.

Source: St Hill, 2000

The Commonwealth Secretariat exercise, for reasons of resource constraints and the limitations in the existing body of work, focused on the analysis of public expenditure. This involved the separation and examination of government expenditures in the following three categories (Sharp and Broomhill, 1990):

A. *Gender specific expenditures:* these are allocations to programmes that are specifically targeted to groups of women, men, boys or girls, such as programmes on men's health (e.g., prostate cancer) or violence against women.

B. *Expenditures that promote gender equity within the public service:* these are allocations to equal employment opportunities, such as programmes that promote equal representation of women in management and decision-making across all occupational sectors, as well as equitable pay and conditions of service. This is distinct from programmes that promote the employment of equal numbers of women and men.[2]

C. *General or mainstream expenditures:* these are allocations that are not covered in the two categories above (A & B). The analysis focuses on the differential impact of the sectoral allocations on women and men, boys and girls. Although the analysis is challenging due to the lack of gender-disaggregated data in many instances, these expenditures are also the most critical because more than 99 per cent of government expenditure usually falls into this category.

The six broad categories of tools[3] that the Commonwealth GRB initiative has used to integrate a gender analysis into the budget are:

- Gender-Aware Policy Appraisal
- Beneficiary Assessments
- Public Expenditure Incidence Analysis
- Gender-disaggregated Analysis of the Budget on Time Use
- Gender-Aware Medium-Term Economic Policy Framework
- Gender Responsive Budget Statement

The Rationale for Gender Responsive Budgets

A gender responsive budget is an important mechanism for ensuring greater consistency between economic goals and social commitments. Some of the more compelling justifications

2 Having equal numbers of men and women does not prevent a situation where, for example, with 100 employees, the 50 men are managers and the 50 women are secretaries.

3 See the Annex to the section by Diane Elson, above.

are presented below, taking into account economic, political, legal and rights-based factors, including mandates from the various international agreements and declarations to which Commonwealth members and other states are signatories. These justifications have been listed individually below, although the subsequent discussions will indicate that they are often interlinked and mutually reinforcing:

1. Economic Efficiency
2. Good Governance
3. Right to Information
4. International Development Commitments and Commonwealth Mandates
5. Gender Mainstreaming

Economic Efficiency

The most widely used argument for undertaking GRB initiatives is that they lead to a more efficient use of resources. Gender analyses of government budgets are crucial for improved targeting, thereby avoiding 'false economies', that is, where attempts to reduce or contain financial costs in one sector may transfer or perpetuate actual costs in terms of time use for individuals and groups, and lower their overall productivity (Elson, 2000). In such cases, actual savings do not result for individuals and groups, particularly women. Similarly, growth has to be accompanied by the reduction of inequalities in order for sustained prosperity and human development to occur. The complementarity of efficiency with equity, referred to as 'new growth theory' (or endogenous growth theory), advocates for state investment in broad infrastructure (financial, physical, technological, educational, environmental and social) that supports and 'crowds-in' private sector responses to achieve this (Palmer, 1995). The framework for GRB analysis involves the examination of inputs, activities, outputs and impacts of government interventions and provides comprehensive feedback on the effectiveness and efficiency of public expenditure. This results in a more optimal use of limited public resources and improved budgetary performance.

Financial cutbacks in medical services in hospitals may reduce provisions for post-operative recovery, resulting in patients being discharged early from hospitals and into 'community-care'. This transfer of the burden of convalescent care to the community and, in turn, to the women in the home, can have a knock-on effect as it places addition burdens on women, often forcing them to be absent from paid employment and lowering their productivity.

Source: Elson, 2000

Research on human development and the reduction of poverty has established beyond doubt that, while distinctions have to be made between rich and poor households, there is a need for assessments of individual well-being within each unit. This is because there are differential impacts of public expenditure on individual members within households, with the more vulnerable having less access to available resources. Crucially, GRB initiatives provide an opportunity to evaluate not simply the nature and extent of the paid economy but also to evaluate the unpaid work, in particular the provision of care which individuals undertake, both in the community and in households. The recognition of this interaction enables policy-makers to avoid 'false economies' and the loss of output.

The new gender-aware approaches to macroeconomic analyses have three basic underpinnings:

- *The recognition that economic institutions may not be intrinsically gender neutral, but instead may bear and transmit gender biases through their assumptions and practices.*
- *The recognition that the cost of reproducing and maintaining the labour force in a society includes the critical contribution from the unpaid economy and that, to make the value of unremunerated work visible, macroeconomics has to be reoriented and redefined.*
- *An understanding that gender relations are primary social determinants in the division of labour, and thus that the distribution of employment, income, wealth and productive inputs have important macroeconomic implications.*

Source: Elson and Cagatay, 1999

There is a large body of research which demonstrates the ways in which macroeconomic policies and institutions which are not gender sensitive not only impact negatively on women relative to men but, through the perpetuation and exacerbation of gender inequality, also impact negatively on the achievement of set macroeconomic goals.[4]

The role of the state, as previously mentioned, goes beyond that of addressing market distortions: It has primary responsibility for redressing inequalities and issues of distributive justice. This position expands on the poverty-reduction framework for pro-poor policies in market operations that Poverty Reduction Strategy Papers (PRSPs) advocate. It also considers the contributions and costs of citizens not directly engaged with the productive economy. When incorporated with gender issues, and those of exclusion and marginalisation, this approach provides a more comprehensive analysis for targeting purposes.

UK Treasury officials, in a meeting with the Women's Budget Group, expressed an interest in gender responsive budgets in terms of the relationship between the effectiveness of budgetary measures to end child poverty and the budgetary measures that reduce gender inequality.

Source: UK Women's Budget Group, 2001

To inform policy, it is important to have gender-disaggregated data to show how men and women may be differently affected. These gender differences are important for understanding other policy concerns, such as the characteristics of the poor, in order to enhance efforts to reduce poverty through targeted spending.[5]

4 For a comprehensive discussion, see *World Development*, Vol. 23 (11) (1995) and Vol. 28 (7) (2000); Beneria, L. (1995); Elson, D. (ed.) (1991); Palmer , I. (1991); Sen G. and Grown, C (1988).

5 There is a large body of literature that demonstrates the ways in which benefit incidence approaches and gender disaggregation exercises can be readily incorporated into a methodology (Demery, 1998).

Good Governance

While 'good governance' is defined in different ways, it is primarily considered to be a process of improving opportunities for the delivery of goods and services to the people in a fair, just, effective and responsible way. Gender responsiveness is essential to the key features of good governance: transparency, accountability and participation. The analysis of gender issues, the participation of women as well as men in decision-making processes at all levels and the recognition by institutions of women's rights and needs are all central to good governance and are strong features in GRB initiatives.

Growth and equity need not be contradictory goals. While dominant economic growth models do not emphasise the link between economic growth and human development, evidence suggest that investments in improving skills and meeting basic social needs can contribute to sustained economic growth (Klasen, 1999). However, while there have been examples of countries managing to improve human development in situations of economic hardship, it is usually not possible to sustain human development without economic growth. It is only in instances where the linkages between the two have been reinforced with policies and procedures for good governance that economic growth has effectively improved human development. In this respect, GRB initiatives can be an important instrument of such governance.

Clearly good governance is a prerequisite for, and an essential component of, sustainable human development. By promoting accountability and transparency, it has also had a direct as well as an indirect impact upon the reduction of opportunities and incentives for corruption. Fostering these important aspects and values of good governance in the public domain requires a more participatory approach in the design, implementation and evaluation of projects and programmes. This strengthens the mechanisms for inputs of and reactions by communities and associations of local beneficiaries and users, particularly women in the case of GRB work (Dollar *et al.*, 1999a). GRB initiatives within governments have contributed to these processes.

Gender responsive governance depends upon dynamic and active partnerships in the social and political forums that elaborate and redefine public policy. If these strategic partnerships are to jointly uphold the right of citizens to participation, information and accountability, they need to include civil society, especially women's networks at grassroot, local, national and global levels. This requires building alliances and includes:

- Strengthened role of women's groups in negotiation processes at different levels.
- Identification of new allies and partners, especially supportive men.
- Enhanced donor and developmental agencies support.
- Improved access to public information through the mass media and new information and communication technologies.
- Increased national capacities, in particular national mechanisms for promoting gender equality and the empowerment of women to participate in policy analysis and dialogue.
- Enhanced accountability and participation at the local level, by giving greater importance to decentralisation processes and decentralised development cooperation.
- Strengthened capacity for gender analysis and governance.

The Right to Information

The demands for transparency and accountability have also been articulated in debates regarding the right to information as a global public good. The key idea posed is that knowledge is a critical component in economic production, and the degree of access to it represents one of the main divides between rich and poor. Increasingly too, information and the tools for manipulating and communicating it are 'controlled' or owned by individuals or corporations rather than being public goods available to everyone. It is crucial to recognise that without a strong and sustained demand for public sector information, accountability initiatives and anti-corruption strategies are likely to fail.

The quantity and quality of available information is changing dramatically every day in every country in the world. Citizens are gaining greater and greater access to information, too. And perhaps, most importantly, the spread of information is making accountability and transparency facts of life for any free government. The consent of the governed – the conditions of any free society – must be an informed, enlightened consent.

UN Secretary-General Kofi Annan, Global Knowledge

Freedom of information – and, more specifically the right to seek, receive and impart information – is a fundamental human right; indeed a prerequisite for many others.

UNESCO, Many Voices, One World

GRB initiatives require the availability of accurate records and of gender-disaggregated data, which can help support other measures designed to improve public expenditure accountability. They are, therefore, pioneering experiments for encouraging open government and maintaining an informed civil society. At the same time, they provide a monitoring tool and framework for objective comparison of the developmental achievements of governments gained through public expenditure.

A mass-based organisation called Mazdoor Kisan Shakti Sanghathan (Movement for the Empowerment of Peasants and Workers) or MKSS, in one of India's poorest areas, seems to have given new meaning to the demand for the right-to-information in the context of development. Since 1990 MKSS has sought to ensure transparency and accountability in development projects of the government at the panchayat *(the lowest local government unit). They now convene public hearings* (jan sunwayi)*, which elected officials and local government officials are invited to attend, to address discrepancies in official records of expenditure and villagers' own experiences as labourers on public-works projects, as applicants for anti-poverty schemes and as consumers in ration shops.*

Source: Jenkins and Goetz, 1999

International Commitments and Commonwealth Mandates

There has been growing recognition that the processes of globalisation are having varied impacts upon different groups and communities. Following a decade when stabilisation and macroeconomic adjustment were the dominant priorities, poverty reduction has reappeared on the international agenda and leading multilateral and bilateral agencies have adopted poverty reduction as their overarching objective and the benchmark for measuring performance. The Washington consensus, which influenced much of the thinking in the Bretton-Woods Institutions in the 1990s and the structural adjustment programmes thereafter, was generally unable to restore growth, despite relative success in instilling fiscal discipline. The emerging view is that macroeconomic policies need to be accompanied by a set of social policies that target social and gender equality, poverty reduction, environmental regeneration and basic labour standards, amongst other areas.

The Commonwealth commitment to gender equality was declared by Heads of Government at Harare in 1991 as a fundamental principle. This was reaffirmed by Heads in their endorsement of the *Commonwealth Plan of Action on Gender and Development* (and its update, 'Advancing the Commonwealth Agenda for Gender Equality into the New Millennium, 2000–2005') and the *Beijing Platform for Action* from the UN Fourth World Conference on Women (1995). The promotion of gender equality by Commonwealth member states reflects that governments, as the representatives of the democratic will of the people, the principal architects of development strategies and the signatories to these global declarations, have primary responsibility for implementing initiatives to promote gender equality.

However, there has been a tendency for commitments to gender to flounder for lack of resources. Many governments desire to do more but are restricted by limited resources. GRB initiatives, by supporting the targeting and effective use of those resources that are already available, provide a practical strategy to build upon the global consensus on the priority of gender equality. Gender responsive budgets allow for increasing outcomes within the confines of available resources. They could also provide an initial step in the monitoring of the implementation and impacts of programmes at the local, national, regional and global levels and the nature of participatory decision-making, thereby strengthening accountability and responsibility for upholding the commitments made to goals of poverty reduction and gender equality.

GRB initiatives, by directly linking stated policy commitments to the distribution, use and generation of public resources, offer a way of enhancing government's ability to respond to gender issues within a context of fiscal propriety. The Women's Budget Initiative in South Africa, a coalition of parliamentarians supported by civil society agencies, provided data on the impact of government programmes on women and has encouraged the introduction of more gender-sensitive programmes in many sectors including education, land distribution, water and sanitation.

Source: Budlender, 1996

Gender Mainstreaming

GRB initiatives were designed as an application of gender mainstreaming, the current international approach to promoting equality between women and men. The Commonwealth's unique and innovative contribution, *Gender Management Systems* (GMS), is a holistic and system-wide approach to gender mainstreaming developed by the Commonwealth Secretariat for use in governments in partnership with other stakeholders, including civil society and the private sector.[6] Along these lines, the Organisation for Economic Cooperation and Development (OECD) held a ministerial conference on gender mainstreaming in November 2000 to illustrate how it 'promotes strong economies, competitiveness and growth'.

6 The GMS, a comprehensive network of structures, mechanisms and processes to enable governments and other organisations to integrate gender equality through all policy-making, planning and activities, is being introduced to Commonwealth countries through regional workshops and has been offered directly, through capacity building missions, to 13 Commonwealth governments.

As budgets involve all government ministries and departments, GRB initiatives provide a practical opportunity for government officials across ministries to develop skills to apply gender tools to their work programmes. In addition, the focus on engaging Ministries of Finance, given their pre-eminent role in budget management, introduces gender issues into the core of both government operations and finance management.

The Government of St Kitts and Nevis requested that the Commonwealth Secretariat provide technical assistance to implement a gender responsive budget initiative following the previous implementation of the Commonwealth's GMS.

Source: Ministry of Finance, 1998

The Commonwealth in seeking to create an environment conducive to its commitments to economic development, gender equality and good governance, advocates for gender responsive budgets to be implemented to further these goals.

Commonwealth Country Experiences

Attempts to apply a gender analysis to government budgets began in Australia in 1984. The exercise was undertaken by the government and coordinated by the Office of the Status of Women. At its height, it was integrated into the budgetary preparations of the federal and all state and territorial budgets. Canada followed in 1993, with a one-off non-governmental organisation (NGO) exercise which focused on the reallocation of defence spending to social services. The South African initiative began in 1994. In 1995 the Commonwealth Secretariat sought to build on the successes of these pioneering initiatives and began a five-country pilot project.

GRB initiatives have now been implemented in forty countries, nearly half of them in the Commonwealth, at national, provincial or local levels. These Commonwealth countries include Australia, Barbados, Botswana, Canada, Fiji Islands, Kenya, Malawi, Mauritius, Mozambique, Namibia, South Africa, Sri Lanka, St Kitts and Nevis, Tanzania, Uganda, UK, Zambia and Zimbabwe.[7] Many of these initiatives have been exploratory and, while this evaluation provides a number of lessons that can be used to develop and implement such programmes on a wider scale, the specific economic impacts are still difficult to determine.

The nature of GRB initiatives varies from country to country. Some were coordinated and led by governments and others by civil society agencies. In a small number of countries, a parallel and complementary dual-track approach, both government and civil society activities, was used, with connections between the separate initiatives. Based on the responsibility of the executive and legislative branches for national budgets, the Commonwealth Secretariat promotes government-led initiatives, implemented in collaboration with civil society groups.

The number of participating countries, donor agencies and other supportive actors involved in the programme continues to increase.[8] The groundswell of support is a consequence of the capacity of GRB initiatives to advance the process of gender equality in a tangible and practical way, that is, by linking objectives related to gender equality directly to public resource allocation and use. A further strength of the programme is the central involvement of the state, in collaboration with civil society institutions, in the design and implementation of country initiatives.

The role of different country-level actors and the strategies and

7 The Commonwealth Secretariat coordinated the implementation of programmes in Barbados, Fiji Islands, St Kitts and Nevis, South Africa and Sri Lanka. The programme in the Fiji Islands was postponed in light of their suspension from the Councils of the Commonwealth. The Government of Belize has submitted a proposal to the Commonwealth Secretariat for technical assistance and the Government of Malaysia is considering beginning an initiative.

8 Initiatives in developing countries have also been supported by a number of agencies and bodies including the Asian Development Bank (ADB), the German Technical Cooperation Agency (GTZ), the Swedish International Development Cooperation Agency (SIDA), the Swiss Development Corporation, the UK Department for International Development (DFID), the governments of Denmark, the Netherlands and Norway, UNDP and UNIFEM. The World Bank has in its gender publications promoted the idea of GRB analysis, and particularly the models used in South Africa and Tanzania. The UN European Economic Commission also has plans to support work on gender and budgets and, in particular, to develop initiatives in Eastern Europe.

components in the programme are examined below in order to identify what worked but also to indicate what changes may be required to ensure greater effectiveness and the sustainability of the programme.

The Role of the Ministry of Finance

One of the features of the Commonwealth Secretariat's GRB initiative is the direct engagement and coordination of the programme by the Ministry of Finance (incorporating the budget department). The Commonwealth Secretariat's gender responsive budgets in Barbados, the Fiji Islands, South Africa, Sri Lanka and St Kitts and Nevis were led by Ministries of Finance, which provided the most strategic way forward for the following reasons:

1. The Ministry of Finance has the requisite technical expertise to implement this process within the government.

2. For GRB initiatives to be effective, they have to be implemented within the context of the annual budget cycle and the medium-term expenditure framework, which are usually coordinated by the Ministry of Finance.

3. Within a framework of gender mainstreaming, the ministry/department responsible for the programme area, in this case the budget office, is encouraged to take the lead on the implementation of the programme.

The initiative in Sri Lanka, coordinated by the Department of National Planning in the Ministry of Finance, brought together government officials across a wide range of departments. An Inter-Ministerial Steering Committee, including representatives of the Ministry of Women's Affairs and Department of Census and Statistics, met each month to assess progress. Findings and implications were presented in six sectoral reports at two workshops for officials from key line ministries along with NGOs, research institutes and donor agencies.

Source: Department of National Planning, 2000

The Role of the Ministry Responsible for Women's Affairs

Although the participation of the Ministry Responsible for Women's Affairs is vital, it will tend to play a supportive rather than a leadership role because of a lack of the requisite technical skills and resources to coordinate the implementation of the programme. Rather than being a criticism, this recognises the severe financial, human and technical resource constraints these Ministries often face.[9] Alternatively, given the cross cutting nature of these Ministries' mandates, instead of programme implementation they may also see their role more as advocates and catalysts to mainstream gender and encourage action within government as a whole on gender equality.

The Role of the Political Directorate

Budgetary resource allocations are inherently political. Given the scarcity of resources and the competing demands that exist, politicians have to establish strategic priorities based on their understanding of the needs and preferences of their key constituencies. The effectiveness and success of GRB initiatives, therefore, depends on the degree of political support that the process is able to secure from the highest levels of government: from Ministers of Finance and Ministries Responsible for Women's Affairs and, given the cross-cutting nature of the initiative, from their Cabinet colleagues.

The Minister of Finance of Mauritius, in his endorsement of the initiative's aim 'at influencing resource allocations that reduce gender discrepancies and inequalities', supported the use of the budget 'to translate gender-oriented policies into concrete action programmes'. Mauritius began work on gender responsive budgets in February 2000.

Source: Ministry of Finance, 1999

9 The 2000 Report by the Commonwealth Secretary-General to the Sixth Meeting of Ministers Responsible for Women's Affairs, held in India, indicated that the need for additional resources was 'one area which has not shown improvement since 1996 (when the previous Ministerial Meeting was held) where 76 per cent of ministries indicated that their human resources were inadequate.'

The Role of Lawmakers

Institutional arrangements to maintain fiscal discipline can range from formal constitutional restraints on aggregate expenditure through formal laws to public commitments by the Executive. Within the context of GRB initiatives, the thrust towards incorporating the State has been to engage the Legislative as well as the Executive branch. Although it is ministers and officials of national or sub-national governments who draw up budgets, representative institutions such as parliaments, local councils or district assemblies have an important role to play in the budgetary processes through debates and, in some situations, their powers to amend budgets. The focus on lawmakers is also important given the recent efforts towards strengthening governance through increased accountability and participation. In Uganda, for example, the GRB initiative emerged as an outside government exercise, the result of collaboration between the Parliamentary Women's Caucus and the Forum for Women in Democracy (FOWODE), an NGO. In 1997, the Women's Caucus embarked on a three-year initiative to examine the effect on women of shifts in public expenditure arising out of structural adjustment packages. After the first year, the initiative was extended to the district level.

The formal process of budget formulation may find additional support and greater success through the active engagement of the elected representatives who, using gender sensitive measurements, could support and monitor the attainment of economic and social goals specified in the budget.[10]

The Role of Civil Society Groups

Civil society participation is important in the Commonwealth. At the 1999 Commonwealth Heads of Government Meeting in Durban, Heads declared that, 'people-centred development implied that people must be directly involved in the decision-making process and in the implementation of development plans and programmes through their own organisations'. They

10 International Budget Project (IBP) and the Inter-Parliamentary Union (IPU) are working to increase economic literacy among members of parliaments.

The South Africa Women's Budget Initiative has from its inception been an alliance forged among those parliamentarians who, entering parliament for the first time in 1994, were eager to continue their work on gender and other forms of discrimination. The parliamentarians and members of the Joint Standing Committee on Finance came together with two NGOs who had the expertise and time necessary to collect information, undertake the research and produce the analysis. For their part, the parliamentarians were able to provide access to information, focus in terms of key political issues and a strong advocacy voice.

Source: Budlender, 2000

noted the significance of civil society involvement in empowering people to benefit from globalisation and in contributing towards the goals of the elimination of poverty, equal opportunity and the fair distribution of resources (Commonwealth Secretariat, 1999).

Civil society groups engaged in GRB initiatives, primarily women's organisations and NGOs, usually support the process by identifying social needs and by examining the budget in terms of the use of public funds to address social concerns. They have also used the analyses as advocacy tools to encourage governments to create a synergy between their economic policy goals and their social policy commitments. Policy research institutes and academic centres have contributed to research and the development of the tools used in the analysis.

Since a government's budget directly or indirectly affects the life of all its citizens, it is important for all levels of civil society to be consulted. Frequently, it is people with modest means and little political influence who are most affected by budget decisions. For these groups, income assistance and social insurance programmes are especially important to their family's well-being, and expenditure in areas such as education and health have a considerable effect on their current vitality and future prospects. Given women's social reproductive roles and their over-representation among the poor, there is a direct interest in examining the effects of budget policies, allocations and expenditures on women. In the UK, the Treasury has begun a process of consultation with the UK Women's Budget Group on the impact of taxes and state benefits on women.

The Women's Budget Group in the UK now has regular meeting with the Treasury to review existing and planned policies and programmes. Such meetings are consistent with the UK Government's commitments to mainstreaming gender and consultation with and involvement of the greater public in policy formulation. The Women's Budget Group has commented on a number of programmes including the Working Families Tax Credit.

Sources: Himmelweit, 2000 and Elson, 2000

The *World Development Report 2000/01*, in the section on 'making state institutions more responsive to poor people', speaks of the need to create decentralised mechanisms for broad participation in the delivery of public services. Towards this end, the report underscores the value of engaging civil society and, specifically, working with NGOs. This is because the 'social and educational background of many NGO staff enables them to interact easily with the staff of national institutions, and they can help create bridges between these institutions, external agencies, and grassroots organisations' thereby contributing to transparency and sustainability.

Participatory approaches to budgets – pro-environment, pro-poor and pro-gender – are being pioneered in some countries, reflecting a new understanding of governance, democracy and policy-making processes. In these exercises, participation means incorporating the voices of those whose needs are often ignored. The Tanzanian Gender Networking Programme (TGNP), a national NGO, is currently providing assistance to the Government to incorporate a gender perspective into their national budget.

In the 2000/01 budget process in Tanzania, gender concerns were included in the guidelines. All Ministry, Department and Agency (MDA) budget submissions were mandated to include a gender focus. The Tanzanian Gender Networking Programme was commissioned by the Ministry of Finance to mainstream gender into six sectors of the budget.

Source: Tanzanian Gender Networking Programme, 2000

Decentralisation and Devolved Management

The process of budget formulation, monitoring and appraisal has traditionally been a function of the central budget office or the Ministry of Finance. The budget office functioned as a central command and control post, specifying the levels of expenditure, monitoring compliance with regulations, ensuring that the inputs are those agreed in the budget and intervening when deemed appropriate (Shick, 2000; Sen, 1999).

However, the recent moves towards fiscal decentralisation in both developed and developing countries mark a movement towards more broad-based participation and may transform the central governments' decision-making role (Yilmaz, 2000). Recommendations are for shifts in the decision-making authority from central institutions to line agencies and from headquarters to subordinate units and field offices. In order to reorient its managerial role, the central budget office would have to transform some of its approaches towards its basic functions; the ways in which the totals are controlled, priorities established and efficiency sought would have to be conducted in an environment of devolved management. This is a crucial entry point for GRB initiatives that can facilitate ways in which such devolution can be undertaken with mechanisms of participation and accountability in place for public expenditure impact assessments.

Several countries, including South Africa, Tanzania and Uganda, have already initiated GRB work at the sub-national level. Local level interventions are necessary since functions and budgets are increasingly being decentralised, often under advice from multilateral and bilateral institutions.

Lessons Learned: Opportunities and Challenges

The review of the outcomes of GRB initiatives should be seen within the context of the programme having recently been developed and the need to devise new and more sustainable strategies based on lessons learned. Nonetheless, there have been a number of positive benefits, which should be highlighted:

- an enhanced ability to determine the real value of resources targeted towards gender-specific groups;
- the challenge to notions of 'gender-neutrality' of many policies and programmes; and
- the strengthening of the collection and analysis of gender-disaggregated data.

Significant factors such as the leading role of the state, especially the budget office and the policy-makers, as well as the incorporation of civil society institutions, are proving of critical significance and need to be focused on in a structured way. Tools for the gender analysis of revenue measures also need to be developed. Gender responsive budgets are proving to be crucial tools for increasing the effectiveness of resource use, strengthening economic management and advancing the pursuit of gender equality.

Opportunities

1. ***GRB analysis provides the opportunity to objectively determine the real value of resources targeted to women, men, boys and girls.*** The emphasis is on analysing the mainstream core government programmes. Since budget allocations to gender-specific programmes do not normally exceed one per cent of total government spending, high-profile programmes such as national gender plans or interventions for girl's education or against domestic violence should not be interpreted as evidence of an overall gender responsiveness in a government budget (Budlender and Sharp, 1998).
2. ***The GRB process uncovers the scarcity of gender-disaggregated statistical data and information on the situation of women and men, which is a particular constraint to effective programme design and implementation.*** Regarding the gender debate in the Caribbean, a country coordinator of the GRB initiatives in the region noted that 'officials in government are not always aware enough of the [gender] issues nor seized with the empirical data surrounding the subject to make an

informed comment or contribute to the process [of addressing gender concerns]. This not withstanding, comments abound and there is a massive debate' (Dalrymple, 2000).

The strength of the South African GRB initiative was its linkage to the collection of gender-disaggregated data by the national statistical office. The introduction to the government statistical publication Women and Men in South Africa, *notes that: 'gender statistics are urgently required. The Office of the Status of Women, the Commission on Gender Equality, and the gender desks within national departments ... need information on the situation of women and men. All spheres of government need gender-disaggregated information to fulfil their planning functions, and as time goes by ... to measure whether policies and programmes are succeeding in addressing gender inequalities.*

Source: Budlender, 1998

3. ***Given that the budget is a paramount, system-wide and participatory process, GRB initiatives provide the opportunity for the key officials in the government to get exposure to a form of easily applicable gender training.*** Gender responsive budgets provide the most practical opportunity for government officials to understand that nearly all government policies have gender impacts and that the perceived notion of 'gender neutrality' is very often a result of inadequate information or analysis. The Commonwealth GRB training focuses on individuals considered strategic in terms of their institutional role in programme and budget formulation: senior officials, policy advisers, planning officers, budget analysts and information/data managers.

A review of the Australian women's budget process indicated that one of the purposes of the initiative was 'to build into each department a clear awareness that everything they do, every dollar they spend, has an impact on women – and that that impact is very often different for women than for men'.

Source: Sharp and Broomhill, 1990

4. ***GRB initiatives examine equal opportunities in the public service.*** The component of GRB initiatives that examines public sector employment, as a category of budget expenditure, is likely to reveal unequal opportunities in the public service even in countries where women have equal access to tertiary education and strong career prospects in that field.

5. ***GRB initiatives have the capacity to address other social concerns.*** In South Africa the research into the impact of budgets and the distribution of resources focused not only on gender, but issues of race as well. Vivienne Taylor (1999) suggests that the annual budget cycle 'could include criteria to measure how the budget responds to race, gender, caste/class [age] and other social disparities'. The process has the potential of promoting greater effectiveness and transparency in decision-making on expenditure allocations or revenue measures as it adds the practical and human dimension of 'who will benefit' to the questions of 'what to do' and 'how to do it'.

Challenges

1. ***The need for political support.*** Although the Ministries of Finance approved the Commonwealth Secretariat's initiatives, there has only been a moderate response from governments in terms of political commitment to the process. While Ministers Responsible for Women's Affairs have been strong advocates, their limited capacity to address macroeconomic issues and their lack of political influence in many governments constrains their ability to mobilise the necessary support. There is a critical need for support by the Ministers of Finance and those in the sectoral ministries.

2. ***While the Ministry of Finance is best placed currently to implement GRB initiatives, its staff very often regard gender issues as the remit of social sector ministries. They also find difficulty in making the link between gender and economic policy issues.*** This uncertainty among finance officials is possibly the most significant

factor in determining whether GRB initiatives become a sustainable process within governments. Work towards integrating social policy issues into public expenditure training and management processes needs to be expanded.

3. ***Generally, government officials lack gender knowledge and expertise and require additional gender sensitisation and training.*** Although many countries are implementing gender-training programmes, this training is usually generic and lacking in practical application for effective knowledge transfer. The practical outcome is for officials to remain ambivalent and for junior staff to be allocated responsibility for gender related activities. This then has little impact as the latter have neither the experience nor the authority to commit resources to these initiatives. This absence of high-level commitment is compounded by the rotation of junior staff, which affects continuity.

4. ***The need to analyse revenue impacts.*** To balance the expenditure-oriented analysis of GRB initiatives, there is a need to examine the gender impacts of revenue-raising measures. A serious constraint to gender and revenue analysis has been a lack of data. Official statistics reflecting gender breakdowns are not readily available, and although the revenue offices collect gender-disaggregated data on individual personal income taxpayers, data is not collected in most countries when it comes to indirect taxes. Even when data is available, there is usually no perceived need to incorporate a gender dimension into tax incidence analysis.

5. ***The need for effective programme coordination.*** The wide range tasks associated with the implementation of this initiative at the country level – training, the establishment of coordination structures and implementation processes, research, monitoring and the sharing of information – requires a significant commitment to coordination. Attempts to add these responsibilities to the existing duties of a government official or group of officials, especially without a sense of priority, has not been effective. Consideration needs to be given to ensuring that country programme coordination is structured in such a way that the necessary

skills, time, commitment, participatory mechanisms and decision-making responsibility are available to successfully implement the initiative.

6. ***The issue of continuity is important as the application of a gender analysis to government budgets takes time.*** Although the budget is an annual process and therefore results from efforts to integrate a gender analysis can be available relatively quickly, to conduct gender analyses of all ministries/departments and to implement the results of the analyses requires a longer period of time. This is usually to accommodate capacity building, competing demands on staff time and the shortage of available expertise. In South Africa the process of conducting a gender analysis of all the portfolios took three years.

7. ***The minimal budgetary power of many lawmakers has been a limitation.*** In many countries, there is an absence of legislative responsibility to amend planned government expenditure or revenue, while in others the situation can be one in which, for political reasons, the budgets are approved without significant critical debate.

8. ***Government and civil society collaboration.*** The best condition for a sustainable initiative is a process of dialogue and complementarity between the government-led initiative and civil society activities, ensuring that a synergy occurs between the aims, expertise and capabilities of each group. This enhances the accountability, efficiency and effectiveness of GRB initiatives. Generally, both governments and civil society agencies have reservations about working together. This is due, in many instances, to historical tensions between the two groups regarding perceived differences in goals and objects, issues of mandates and representativeness, concerns over confidentiality, or varying time-horizons. Nonetheless, experience suggests that to ensure effective implementation and sustainability of gender responsive budgets, there needs to be leadership by the government and, where possible, the involvement of civil society agencies in the design and implementation of the programme.

9. ***Identifying the role of external agencies.*** Donor institutions and development agencies function best as

catalysts for GRB initiatives, providing technical and logistical support. It is important to reiterate the primacy of local ownership of these initiatives and to highlight the importance of local control in terms of the programme's goals and objectives. In seeking to avoid a dependency on external agencies to implement the programme at the country level, the Commonwealth Secretariat has sought to engage local consultants and ensure that local capacity building and skill transfers takes place.

Future Programme Directions

Efficient and effective processes are being developed to improve the efficacy of GRB initiatives as part of a strategy to increase collaboration between governments and civil society agencies, increase the access of vulnerable groups to resources, goods and services, and improve the rate and distribution of the benefits of economic growth. The new and enhanced programme will continue to promote the following principles:

- *Country ownership:* government commitment and leadership and broad country ownership are critical for effective formulation and implementation of GRB initiatives;
- *Participation:* citizens are not only beneficiaries of development but also agents of development. Where development objectives are to be met through the budget, public expenditure management should involve wide participation in the process. This might include local government authorities, traditional rulers, civil society groups, economic and social research institutes, NGOs, community based organisations and donor agencies.
- *Transparency:* transparency of the consultative, analytic and outcomes processes at the national, provincial and local levels builds trust, ownership and support among civil society and other stakeholders;
- *Sustainability:* processes that build on existing budgetary and public expenditure mechanisms and experiences arising out of the good practices of GRB initiatives are most likely to be institutionalised and sustained over time; and

◊ *Continuous improvement:* gender responsive budgets are iterative processes of consultation, participation, planning, implementation and evaluation against set goals, objectives, indicators and benchmarks. The regular review and updating of process based on emerging experiences will be a critical factor in improving the design and implementation of the programme and strengthening its impacts.

Partnerships

Following a successful meeting of government representatives and civil society institutions from Commonwealth countries and other development agencies at the Commonwealth Secretariat in April 2000 to evaluate the programme, the Secretariat sought to develop partnerships to strengthen the scope and capacities of GRB initiatives. The new inter-agency partners, the International Development Research Centre (IDRC) and the United Nations Development Fund for Women (UNIFEM), will work with the Commonwealth to support the new thrust of the programme.

The new partners bring unique and critical resources to the work. UNIFEM works towards enhancing the role, capacity and participation of women at all levels: national, regional and international. IDRC seeks to help developing countries find solutions to social and economic problems through research, recognising that equitable and sustainable development requires an understanding of the differential impact of policies on women and men. To support the gender responsive budget analysis, IDRC will be drawing on the diverse capacity of its Micro Impact of Macroeconomic and Adjustment Policies (MIMAP) programme begun in 1990. This connects developing country researchers, policy officials, NGOs and international experts in an effort to design better development policies through research and dialogue.

The Commonwealth Secretariat, IDRC and UNIFEM as partners, along with the Government of Belgium, the Organisation of Economic Co-operation and Development (OECD) and the Nordic Council of Ministers, convened a High Level Conference in October 2001 to share lessons learned and to mobilise political and financial support to meet the increasing demand from governments and civil society to carry out GRB initiatives.

Programme Areas

The programme over the short and medium-term will seek to concentrate on the following areas:

- *Capacity strengthening for governments* at different levels to enhance their ability to allocate public expenditure and collect revenue in a gender equitable way.
- *Capacity building for women,* including parliamentarians and local officials as well as women's organisations, to facilitate their understanding of economic issues towards their participation in budgetary processes.
- *Reorientation of national statistical systems* to gather, compile and analyse gender-disaggregated data for budgetary policy formulation and programme implementation.
- *Monitoring and evaluation* of initiatives through the selection of targets and indicators to assess budgetary inputs and outputs and their impacts on women and men over time.
- *Documentation* of the process and its results in an effort to encourage the sharing of good practices in countries across the Commonwealth and beyond.

As part of its international advocacy and inter-agency collaboration, the Commonwealth Secretariat will continue to share information on and solicit support for the programme with multilateral and bilateral institutions.

Developing Tools for Revenue Analysis

GRB initiatives were conceived as a set of analytical tools, a methodological framework and implementation strategy for use by governments to incorporate a gender perspective into budgetary processes. However, for pragmatic reasons, the initiatives have focused to date primarily on the expenditure allocations. Revenue tools are required for a better understanding of the possible gender impacts of revenue-raising measures, as well as to complement work done on expenditure impacts.

Notions of gender in revenue analysis have been confined largely to distributional effects of tax regimes. Direct taxes, essentially personal income tax, fall more on men because of their higher enrolment in the formal labour force, more senior positions and higher incomes. Indirect taxes, such as value-added or consumption taxes, have a greater impact on poor people, who spend a higher percentage of their income on consumer goods and thus end up paying a larger share of their income on such taxes. Indirect taxes have a greater impact on women because women are disproportionately represented among the poor and make proportionately higher contributions to household consumption budgets.

The development of revenue tools is expected to concentrate on:

Direct/personal income tax: Global income taxes are typically the source of gender bias. This can be in the form of marriage penalties, where couples filing joint returns incur a greater tax liability that if they filed as single individuals, or where tax on the second income in a household begins at a higher that the base rate of tax. Gender bias can also occur when all non-labour income (from assets, savings, property or business) or tax expenditures (subsidies, deductions, exemptions or credits) are allocated to the male spouse only or not available to a married woman who is the sole earner.

In 1991, Malaysia abolished the practice where the income of a married woman was automatically attributed to her husband unless she elected for separate assessment, and replaced it with a system in which husbands and wives are treated as separate taxable units with an option for joint treatment.

In 1995, South Africa abolished the application of a higher rate for single persons and married women than for married men, and changed to a unified rate.

Source: Stotsky, 1996

Indirect/Commodity tax: The current trends towards reducing trade taxes (liberalisation policies) and a demand for greater ease in collection has led to indirect taxes now constituting a larger percentage of tax revenue than direct taxes in many countries. While these taxes may seem to be gender-neutral as they are attached to products and services, they can have significant gender implications, given that women and men tend to use/consume different products/services, and also based on the way in which household income and expenditure is managed and distributed.

User fees: Since the 1980s the number of countries having implemented some form of user fee system has grown considerably and user financing of basic social services has become common practice in many developing countries. Governments have come to see user fees as an alternative to tax-based financing for a range of public services. Efficiency, effectiveness and even equity arguments have been made for applying these charges, yet supporting evidence is limited. There are, however, some disturbing indications from studies of the social costs (reduced utilisation of services among the poor and negative effects on well-being and health) resulting from the introduction of user fees (Esim, 2000).

Other areas: Other tax issues may be examined for possible gender impacts. These include corporate taxes, primarily the granting of incentives to certain sectors as opposed to others; the impact of globalisation, specifically the reduction in customs and trade taxes; and the debt crisis and the fiscal drain of debt servicing.

Tax systems contain a wide range of taxes, including those on personal and corporate income, payroll, goods and services, foreign trade, wealth, gifts and inheritances. Several aspects of taxes are relevant to pro-poor and gender responsive budgets, including:

1. ***Distributional effects of the tax system:*** *What kinds of tax reforms are more beneficial for the poor, for women in poor households or other target groups? Does the tax system take a larger share of income from lower income (regressive) or higher income (progressive) quintiles?*

2. ***The size of the tax base:*** *The base of taxes needs to be large enough to sustain support for key government programmes. The size and effect of tax cuts should be clearly articulated by governments.*

3. ***Tax structure:*** *There needs to be a balance between direct and indirect taxation and between taxes based on income, expenditure (consumption and investment) and resource use.*

4. ***Tax administration:*** *The issues of tax compliance/avoidance/evasion, legitimacy of tax systems/corruption and impact of taxes are also relevant.*

Source: Esim, 2000

Conclusion

GRB initiatives provide a mechanism by which governments, in collaboration with lawmakers, civil society groups, donor and other development agencies, can integrate a gender analysis into fiscal policy and budgets. By integrating social and economic development policy, gender responsive budgets promote the complementarity of growth and equity, reducing areas of trade-off between equality and efficiency. They also strengthen governance processes and provide a strategy for promoting efficient and equitable economic policies as an integral component of national development.

Building on the experience gained from the programme in Commonwealth countries, the Commonwealth Secretariat seeks to consolidate the achievements and increase the implementation of GRB initiatives at the country level. It also seeks to complement work already done on public expenditure by developing measures and tools that can apply a gender analysis to taxation and revenue policies and practices within national and provincial budgets. This work needs to be undertaken in close partnership with other intergovernmental and development agencies and, at the country level, in collaboration with civil society groups, especially women's organisations and economic and social research institutes.

A Global Assessment of Gender Responsive Budget Initiatives

Debbie Budlender

At the time of writing, I had been personally involved in gender responsive budget (GRB) initiatives in more than ten countries, from playing a lead role to making comments on proposals or documents. Given this involvement, I have not attempted an evaluation. Instead, I have tried to provide an honest assessment of experiences and initiatives. The assessment inevitably draws more heavily – particularly in the more nuanced discussions – on the projects I was involved in or on those that have generated reflective material.

Many thanks to Diane Elson, Simel Esim, Guy Hewitt, Randy Spence, Imraan Valodia and Lisa Veneklasen for their useful comments on earlier drafts of this paper, to all the participants in the January 2001 inter-agency meeting in Paris for the discussion, and to Guy Hewitt for his never-ending encouragement and energy. I also thank all those named in the case study section who contributed information about different countries.

Introduction

The following assessment is based on a study of gender responsive budget (GRB) initiatives conducted in over forty countries in different parts of the world by the end of 2000. Pen-sketches of the different country initiatives considered are included as a separate section in this publication. These case studies are referred to in this section to illustrate different points.

The Commonwealth Secretariat commissioned the assessment as a planning document for their partnership with UNIFEM and IDRC. Its structure and the topics covered reflect this origin. It is organised as follows:

- The first part discusses gender responsive budgeting as a strategy for mainstreaming gender into economic policy.
- The second part discusses the goals and objectives of different initiatives.
- The third and fourth parts discuss the roles of international agencies and country-level actors respectively.
- The fifth part talks about the differences between national and sub-national gender budget work.
- The sixth part focuses on implementation strategies.
- The seventh part discusses how GRB work intersects with other developmental programmes.
- Finally, the eighth part proposes some key considerations for the three commissioning partners and others who plan to support GRB work.

A Strategy to Mainstream Gender into Economic Policy

GRB initiatives interact with economic policy at two levels: the macro and the micro. On the macro side, budgets, as fiscal policy instruments, are one of the pillars of the macroeconomic policy of any country. On the micro side, the interaction is more a question of how gender is mainstreamed into the policies and programmes of the economic agencies of governments. The division is simplistic to the extent that the micro occurs within the confines of the chosen macro. Nevertheless, the division provides a basis for discussion. Others have written far more competently on broader economics issues from a gender perspective. This review concentrates on the links as identified in gender responsive budgets (see, Grown *et al.*, 2000; Elson, 1999).

Macroeconomic policy does not generally affect people directly. Instead it influences other levels of government policy which themselves have direct effect. The absence of direct linkages is one of the factors that makes dealing with macroeconomic issues difficult. Another is that, in Gita Sen's words, macro-economics 'carries with it an aura of technical expertise and arcaneness that shrouds its purveyors in a thick veil of mystery'

(1999: 12). This apparent impenetrability is also often associated with gender. Gender responsive budgets thus combine two seemingly obscure areas! Diane Elson (1996) suggests a third factor that makes mainstreaming gender in macroeconomic policy difficult. This is that the range of possible policies and instruments is wider than with other levels of economic policy and potentially more varied across countries than in most subject areas.

It was for some of these reasons that the Commonwealth pilot project on gender and economic policy focused on the budget. The original idea within the Commonwealth was to attempt to engender macroeconomic policy. Later the decision was taken to focus on a 'menu' of budget tools, which would engage economists, finance officials and other economic policy makers in a more practical way. Because the budget takes place annually, this would also allow for completion of the processes of analysis, problem identification, implementation of corrective measures, and monitoring and evaluation of impacts within a relatively short timeframe. Further, the project could be implemented at the country level with relatively modest resources.

The budget was seen as a pragmatic place to start work on engendering macroeconomic policy as gender concerns are more visible in fiscal than in monetary policy. For similar reasons, another body of work has begun to focus on trade as one of the more concrete manifestations of macroeconomic policies. Nonetheless, the GRB approach has been critiqued for focusing too narrowly on budgets without considering the wider macroeconomic picture. One part of this critique is that, by conducting analysis on a sectoral basis, the big picture is missed. A more fundamental critique is that, by not asking questions about the theoretical assumptions underpinning the framing of the budget as a whole, the exercises are reformist rather than transformative. So, for example, the critics would argue that one should rather focus on issues like macroeconomic models, debt, deficits and surpluses before looking at the use of resources within the existing 'envelopes' or sectors. Those involved in GRB initiatives are aware of these problems. In several countries there is an interest in how the parameters of the budget policy and priorities are determined. For example, in Tanzania there are plans to move beyond the budget office and to engage with other parts of the central financial agencies on broader fiscal policy issues.

At the micro-level, several of the initiatives have moved beyond the social sectors, such as education and health, to focus on the economic ones. In particular they have focused on agriculture and industry. One of the difficulties most gender specialists face in analysing the policies and programmes of economic agencies is that these agencies are, with liberalisation, more concerned with regulation (or deregulation) than with programme implementation. With this role, it is much more difficult for them to directly respond to gender and other social concerns. To date, little work has been done on the protective services, despite their importance in respect of issues such as gender violence as well as conflict and war more generally.

Goals and Objectives

The goals and objectives of GRB initiatives differ according to country and the particular stakeholder's interests. For example, the Asia Foundation's motivation to support gender responsive budget work in the Philippines has a broad range of motives. After consultation with government and non-government stakeholders in the country, the aims were formulated so as to achieve more than simply ensuring gender responsive budgets. They were:

- To promote equity, efficiency and effectiveness in government policy and implementation;
- To promote accountability and transparency on the part of government and public representatives, and to minimise corruption;
- To inform and enhance citizen participation and advocacy, particularly for women, by strengthening leverage and tools for policy implementation;
- To encourage citizens' budget literacy and a level of comfort at tracing how much money was allocated to a policy commitment; and
- To contribute to the quality impact of decentralisation

through improved capacity by both officials and community groups.

The initial goals of the South African women's budget initiative, on the other hand, were:

- To develop an alternative set of values and principles which begin to prioritise the socio-economic needs of poor women;
- To provide a critical tool to monitor spending;
- To empower the Standing Committee to oversee government spending;
- To empower government to take responsibility for drawing up gender sensitive budgets; and
- To empower civil society to engage with issues that it has hitherto been excluded from.

A third example comes from UNIFEM, whose description of its interest in GRB initiatives explains how the work fits into each of the Fund's three priority areas. Initially, UNIFEM's support fell under the umbrella of the economic empowerment programme. Subsequent realisation that much of the work involved efforts to empower women's organisations and civil society to participate in policy-making processes resulted in a transfer to the governance programme. However, UNIFEM also sees the work in many countries as falling squarely within the human and economic rights focus (Carr, 2000).

The objectives of the Commonwealth's programme, to give a final example, are to improve the analysis by governments of the effect that budgetary priorities and allocations have on women, men, girls and boys, and to target expenditure and revenue policies in order to offset any undesirable gender-specific consequences. The project was considered a useful entry point to persuade economic policy makers to adopt a more gender sensitive approach. It was also seen as a way of institutionalising the Commonwealth gender mainstreaming approach to policy development and implementation in government (Hewitt and Raju, 1999).

These are only a few examples, but between them they give an idea of the diversity of approaches. Importantly, these examples emphasise that changing what happens within financial ministries is not the sole objective of the programme. The success of the initiatives should, therefore, not be measured only in terms of changes in budgets. The measures of success must, instead, be multi-dimensional.

Further, there are links – both positive and negative – between the different objectives. On the negative side, success in reaching one objective could retard success in reaching another. All budgets are about politics. Stated bluntly, there are those who gain from gender and other inequalities in society, and who are very satisfied with current patterns of resource allocation. Adding gender to other considerations ups the political ante. At present, some of the support for gender or women responsive budget initiatives reflects a welfarist perspective: It is done out of charity or in support of the vulnerable. So, for example, in some discussions around social security, government officials were quick to see the need for programmes to support widows, but slower to see the need to support younger 'able-bodied' women with their responsibilities of bearing and rearing of children.

On the positive side, the many objectives of GRB initiatives mean that they can be attractive to those who would not normally be interested in gender issues. For example, the initiative is able to engage finance and budget officials in a practical way as to how they can address gender inequality in their work.

Yet the question of determining where opportunities for engagement exist is not simple. For example, non-government objectives such as increasing participation in policy making, empowerment and transparency are far more likely to be achieved if the government is open to these ideas. It is no coincidence that many of the initiatives have occurred at a time of social change in particular countries that created more possibilities for their involvement. It could be argued that concentrating on where there are identifiable opportunities avoids confronting those places where the problems are most severe. On the other hand, efforts in a country like Uganda, where the Ministry of Finance is itself promoting many of the ideas, are far more likely to bear fruit. Pragmatism in this case is perhaps better than idealism.

Multilateral and bilateral donors have put governance and related issues such as transparency high on their lists of what the developing countries they support should be doing. When governments profess their own interest in these issues, it is not always clear whether they are doing so to please donors – at least verbally – or because they themselves believe in the benefit. In at least some cases, government officials will overtly or covertly resist taking steps to introduce proposed reforms, sometimes for very legitimate reasons. These include a lack of transparency by the same donors about their own operations. The difficulty is exacerbated by the fact that GRB initiatives are being promoted by international agencies.

In one of the training workshops, when discussing the reasons for undertaking the exercise, an initial response from a participant was the very honest 'because the donors like it'. In another country, a consultant reported that one of the officials had told him that it was not worth spending much effort on gender responsive budget work as it was a passing fad: 'First it was socialism, then performance budgeting, today it is gender'.

McGee *et al.* (2000) reports similar cynicism among government officials about programme shifts of donor agencies, such as the World Bank's from the Comprehensive Development Framework to the Poverty Reduction Strategy Papers. For the officials concerned, the steady flow of new ideas and recommendations from the donors and their consultants usually means significant additional work that might well be later abandoned.

The Role of International Agencies

Multilateral and Bilateral Donors

The country studies reveal that, apart from the partners involved in this initiative (Commonwealth Secretariat, IDRC, and UNIFEM), a number of multi- and bilateral agencies have supported GRB initiatives. These include the Swedish International Development Agency (SIDA), the Swiss Development Corporation, German Technical Cooperation

Agency (GTZ), the UK Department for International Development (DFID), the governments of Denmark, the Netherlands and Norway, and UNDP. The World Bank has, in its gender publications, promoted the idea of gender responsive budget analysis, and particularly the models used in South Africa and Tanzania. The UN European Economic Commission also has plans to support work on gender and budgets and, in particular, to develop initiatives in Eastern Europe.

These agencies are not monolithic in their support for GRB initiatives. In several cases, the specific departments in the agencies that support such initiatives have reported opposition from their colleagues, and particularly from those in the economic affairs sections. Or, where there is support, it is for work that is limited in terms of scope and stakeholders. Within the World Bank, the new managing director, Mamphela Ramphele, was one of the initiators of the South African project and is keen that the Bank should learn more from the experiences. However, apart from a few exceptional individuals, real support seems unlikely to spread all that far beyond a smallish group of converts. In several countries, there are reports of misunderstanding, and sometimes outright resistance, to introducing gender into discussions of macroeconomics, or even the poverty reduction strategies. Where gender is introduced, it is often – as in the Vietnamese case – 'contained' in terms of sector and ambit.

Experience suggests a difference in the way that multilateral and bilateral agencies work on GRB initiatives. In general, the multilaterals seem keener to share information on the activities they are supporting. The bilaterals, on the other hand, are generally reticent. During the research for this assessment, funding agencies in at least two cases said they could not provide any information as it 'belonged' to those they funded. The argument is attractive insofar as it respects ownership. However, the lack of information sharing prevents the different initiatives learning from each other.

In addition to the bilateral agencies, in many countries international NGOs and development agencies make substantial financial and other contributions to projects. However, their contribution seems to be limited in respect of GRB initiatives.

The country profiles provide at least four examples. In South Africa, Oxfam/Novib and the Mott Foundation are loyal funders and the Ford Foundation provided support in the first year. In Mexico, the Ford Foundation provides support. In the Philippines, the Asia Foundation recently began a support programme that it hopes to expand to other countries. In Uganda, the Asia Foundation supported the Debt Network's workshop and Winrock International sponsored the agriculture exercise. The Ford Foundation also provides support to a far larger number of countries in respect of non-gender-focussed budget work.

The international NGOs and foundations are more likely to fund exercises that focus on civil society. Some bilaterals, on the other hand, have been fairly resistant to doing so. In some countries the country agreement may state that the donor agency needs permission from the governments to give money to non-governmental institutions.

Challenges in Donor Financing

Donor support has its drawbacks. One obvious drawback is financial dependency and the dangers this poses to programme sustainability. However, money is necessary if the exercises are to be anything beyond small, one-off interventions. Ironically, developed country initiatives are disadvantaged in this respect as there are far fewer donors active in these countries. But the very extensive role of donors in developing countries also introduces challenges for the budget initiatives. One of these is resistance among both government and non-government players to donor-driven initiatives. For many potential supporters of GRB work, the involvement of the World Bank could discourage participation because their perception of the nature of past Bank activities.

A second challenge arises in respect of methods commonly adopted in donor-funded initiatives. For example, in gender responsive budget exercises and in other interventions, workshops are a popular activity. One reason for this is that they are easily measurable in terms of logical framework planning. Workshops are clearly valid in that they are a good way of spreading new ideas to a group of people. They are particularly valid in the case of GRB initiatives, where one of the important first steps is often basic consciousness-raising around gender issues. However, in many countries the persistence of 'sitting allowances', or other payments to participants, raises questions about the motives of participants in the workshop. Particularly where civil servants earn tiny salaries, participating in workshops can be an end in itself.

There are also questions as to the difference workshops make in relation to what people do in their work. Changing mindsets is the first step, but the ultimate objective is to change what officials do so that things are better for citizens. In at least one country, a supportive high official has stated that it is now time to move beyond awareness rising to empowering officials with concrete tools and practical support.

Many of the GRB training exercises have attempted to respond to the 'output' concern by requiring that there be a concrete 'product', in the form of a report on findings by the different sectors participating and an action plan. In most countries this elicits questions about payment by officials who see this as extra work rather than part of their ordinary workload.

A third challenge arises in respect of consultants. Most bilateral and multilateral funding comes with the expectation that there will be external 'expert' technical assistance in addition to the funds. In some cases there is the further expectation that the experts will come from the funding country. Goetz notes that development agencies generally tend to value information from Western feminists and researchers more than that of women in developing countries. She draws an analogy between this privileging of certain voices and the privileging of economists and economics over development practitioners and theorists (Goetz, 1994:28). Both of these forms of privilege are important to remember in GRB work.

The potential for problems is heightened by the different positions in terms of power and money. On the financial side, the external expert is usually paid substantially more than their local counterpart, if there is one. In terms of power, the external expert will often have divided loyalties, particularly if the employing agency is the funder. But it can also be the case if the government or local partner is the employing agency, as the influence of the funder may be evident behind the scenes.

There is also the issue of the capacity of the consultant. Evaluating expertise in an area like GRB work is extremely difficult. The work is still largely experimental, so there are no simple rules and tools to pass on. Budget work is also a very 'national' issue. While there are many similarities in the way budgets are prepared across countries, and multilateral and bilateral have attempted to standardise approaches, there are still important differences even in the basic format. There are further differences in terms of both theoretical and actual processes of budget making. Added to that are the political considerations.

An experienced 'expert' might know some of the questions to ask, but could also be blinkered because of exposure to other situations. Admittedly, in many countries few gender activists have knowledge about budget matters. On the other hand, they do have an understanding of the gender and political situation in the country. How to bring these different knowledge bases and experiences together optimally is not simple.

Analysing Donor Funds

There has been surprisingly little gendered analysis of donor contributions to country budgets. This is particularly surprising in countries where donors are responsible for very large proportions of government revenue. In South Africa, where donor funds account for less than 2 per cent of the government budget, there have been two analyses. The first formed part of the Fourth Women's Budget and the second was commissioned as part of the government's own development cooperation report. In Mozambique the work within government suggested that documents relating to donor-funded projects could be a rich source of information. In Bangladesh, too, budget analysis of donor funds seems easier than of other funds as donors are most interested in promoting new systems that tell them what is happening in respect of their contributions. However, in countries such as Tanzania, donor funds are among the last aspects planned to be included in new budgeting systems. Government officials have real doubts as to whether they will get access to the information they need.

The need to investigate donor funds is not simply about turning the tables. It also raises important questions about the government's own approach to budgeting. For example, in South Africa the research revealed that a senior Finance official felt that it was not necessary for government to provide much funding for the gender machinery as this area seemed to be a favourite of funders. More broadly, where donor funds form a significant proportion of the budget, how these are used and controlled relates directly to government and country ownership of their own development path.

The Role of Country-Level Actors

At the country level there is a range of different possible players and objectives. The following examination of the role of the different actors recommends that gender responsive budget initiatives should seek to engage as widely as possible.

Government

The government has been the main focus of the Commonwealth Secretariat initiative. And, within governments, the Ministry of Finance – and in particular the budget office – has taken the lead. At the same time, close involvement of the Gender Affairs Ministry has been encouraged in each case. The Ministry of Finance was allocated the lead based on its role in the budgetary process, its overall authority within all governments, and the desire to integrate gender concerns into the mainstream of government activities. The gender ministry usually supported the lead by finance, recognising their own lack of human and technical resources to coordinate the exercises. However, due to the absence of established working relationships between the two ministries, there have been tensions in some countries around a perceived sidelining of the latter. This tension can weaken the initiatives. Firstly, it means that the gender skills located in the Gender Affairs Ministry may not be fully utilised. Secondly, the involvement of this ministry facilitates civil society engagement as in many countries it is the part of government that is more used to working with NGOs.

The Philippines is an exception to the general pattern in that their gender ministry, the National Commission on the Role of Filipino Women (NCRFW), is the clear leader of the GAD budget (see country report). However, even in this case, the NCRFW works hand in hand with the finance institutions. The Philippines experience speaks to the necessity of capacity building for staff of gender affairs ministries if they are to adopt the lead role.

Even where the Ministry of Finance plays a lead role, other ministries are often expected to have a significant part to play. Case studies reveal that most countries have adopted a sectoral approach whereby, at least in the early years, they focus on key agencies. Typically these include health and education, with agriculture a favourite third choice. The sectoral strategy is inevitable given that budgets are constructed sectorally. The choice of education and health is sensible. Firstly, they account for a large proportion of government budgetary expenditure. Secondly, they are generally acknowledged as having particular importance for women and poor people generally. Thirdly, there are many indications that these sectors have often been under attack during structural adjustment. Agriculture and industry are useful choices in emphasising that gender is not only important in the 'soft' social sectors.

Both within the finance institutions and the sectors it is not always clear whom to target. Sen (1999) notes the shift in power from planning agencies to Ministries of Finance. Nevertheless, in some countries the planning agencies are still responsible for key budget decision-making, such as setting the overall budget guidelines. In Tanzania, the Tanzanian Gender Networking Programme (TGNP) recognised this early on and lobbied so as to ensure that paragraphs on the need for gender sensitivity were inserted into the budget guidelines document. Finance ministries themselves will usually be divided into different departments. Thus, although the GRB initiative worked initially with the budget office in Tanzania, there are now plans to extend the work to the departments that are responsible for macroeconomic modelling and for external resources.

Within the sectoral ministries there are variations in terms of who is responsible for budgets. There can also be differences between who has responsibility in terms of compiling figures (budget analysts), developing programme (planning officers) and who has decision-making power (accounting officers). In general, the exercises have mainly involved middle-level technicians such as planners and budget officials. These officials regularly report that, while they fully appreciate the value of a gender responsive budget, as decisions are taken elsewhere, the interventions need to gain the support of more senior officials. In the one hand, this argument almost certainly reflects an effort to pass the buck. On the other, it is invariably true that decision-making takes place in a number of different places. The daunting message for GRB work is the need to target all these different groups in terms of their roles. It may be more helpful to say that the top managers need to understand the need for supporting gender responsive budgets, while the technicians need to understand how to do them.

Further complicating the issue are internal government tensions. With the growing powers of Ministries of Finance, which are often seen as a conduit for restrictions and controls imposed by the multilateral agencies, there can be resistance from sectoral ministries to programmes emanating from Finance. Again, Tanzania serves as an example. In that country, the sectoral officials in many 'non-priority' agencies were unhappy about having to draw up detailed budgets. They felt these were futile because of the cash budgeting and the concomitant centralised decision-making within the Ministry of Finance and Central Bank, under the supervision of the International Monetary Fund (IMF).

Parliament

Many GRB initiatives include among their strategies lobbying and training of parliamentarians, particularly women members, presentations at parliamentary budget hearings and preparation of fact sheets for use by parliamentarians. These strategies might give an appearance of tackling the pinnacle of power but this could be illusory. In many countries, by the time the budget is presented to parliament it is a fait accompli. A

1986 study by the Inter-Parliamentary Union (quoted in Krafchik and Werner, 1999) showed that in well over half the countries studied, parliaments did not have powers to reduce or increase expenditure and revenue. In some cases, spending commences almost immediately, if not before, the budget is formally accepted. In others, parliamentary powers to amend budgets are often limited in scope. In the Philippines, Senator Shahani, a gender activist, introduced the GAD budget resolution through Congress but Congress has had virtually no institutional role since.

Parliament has been an important actor in the South African and Ugandan initiatives. However, after initiating the project in South Africa, the subsequent role of parliament has been relatively weak although there has recently been renewed interest at both national and provincial levels. The weak role of parliamentarians in part reflects the power dynamics that result from different electoral systems and that can limit the potential for lobbying by women MPs. Uganda is a special case here in that the special interests caucus, which is dominated by women, represents the single largest organised group within the parliament. But in both the Ugandan and South African parliaments, participation in the budget initiatives depends heavily on a few key individuals.

Switzerland provides an example of a country in which public representatives currently have an exceptionally high level of budgetary power, which is now being severely reduced with the introduction of New Public Management. In many other countries moves to similar systems of public management are increasing the power of officials in exchange for performance contracts. Such systems will work against calls for increased parliamentary powers.

Krafchik and Wehner (1999) describe the tension as one between 'technicality' (i.e. the bureaucrats) and 'democracy' (the legislature). Without going deeper into the argument, the lesson can be drawn for GRB initiatives that they need to target the bureaucracy as much as – if not more than – the legislature if they hope to change budget policy and outcomes. There are some suggestions that the multi-year budgeting being introduced in many countries (for example, in the form of medium-term expenditure frameworks) will provide greater opportunity and time for parliament and civil society to influence government budgets. In most cases these initiatives are too new to allow for any judgement of the future possibilities.

Civil Society

The Australian GRB exercise is often cited to illustrate the limitations of these initiatives if civil society is not involved. Daram Ghai argues that, more generally, a reason for the limited action by states to implement international and other policy commitments to gender and development is the weakness of public pressure (in Goetz, 1995:ii).

Civil society participation in GRB initiatives is facilitated by a broad common purpose of actors inside and outside government. So, for example, in the South African, Ugandan and Tanzanian initiatives the non-government exercises see themselves as supporting their government's agenda, but pushing a little faster and harder in the directions espoused in their policies on gender equality. In the Philippines, the NCRFW was welcomed as a participant in the Asia Foundation exercise as civil society participants see eye-to-eye with the Gender Affairs Ministry officials.

The analytical approach commonly adopted in many GRB exercises also works best when there is broad agreement between government and those in civil society conducting the analysis. The approach moves from:

- an analysis of the situation of women, men, girls and boys in a given sector, to
- an assessment of the extent to which a policy addresses the (gendered) situation, to
- an assessment as to whether budget allocations are adequate to implement the gender responsive policy, and finally to
- the monitoring of whether and how the budgets are spent and policies and programmes implemented.

This approach will not proceed as far as the budget stage if the policies are found to be inadequate in the second step. When those organising an initiative are questioning government policy, a budget focus at this level is inappropriate.

From within civil society, it is usually NGOs who take the lead. Very often these NGOs are comprised of middle-aged women who are contemporaries of those in government. This facilitates partnerships. Some of the initiatives have drawn on academics to assist with the research, or even training.

The term 'NGO' is broad and obscures important differences between the actors across and within countries. In South Africa, for example, the two core NGOs are policy research organisations. In Mexico, the core NGOs are a policy research organisation and a women's organisation. In Tanzania and Uganda, it is women's or gender organisations that are leading. In the Philippines, the civil society initiative involves two local women's organisations, one 'mixed' people's organisation and a national gender network. Each of the different types of organisations has strengths and weaknesses. Initiatives are probably most successful when the core organisations are able to link up with other 'types' of civil society organisations that complement them.

In Tanzania, the NGOs have worked particularly closely with government on the latter's GRB exercise. One of the more strategic decisions was to allow TGNP facilitators to attend the regular training for budget officials on the new medium-term expenditure framework. By being exposed to this training, TGNP gained important knowledge about how government works and were thus better able to design their training to coincide with this. However, such close collaboration of NGOs and government is not found in many countries. In Tanzania it is the result of trust that was built over time. While governments are often suspicious of NGOs, NGOs similarly often have hesitations about engaging too closely with government. For example, Razavi (1997) points to scepticism among some gender activists about the ability of government bureaucracies to address gender issues adequately. Further, NGOs are concerned about cooption, loss of critical distance, and being used by government or donors. The Tanzanian case study notes TGNP's concerns about this issue (see country profile).

The 'Grassroots'

Few initiatives have succeeded in reaching the 'grassroots'. It is perhaps naïve to expect that grassroots and poor people, usually unorganised or marginalised, can easily be reached and motivated to participate in these initiatives. In general it is the local level initiatives that have gone 'deepest'. The Tanzanian and Uganda initiatives have obtained information from and discussed issues with ordinary people. The proposed Karnataka initiative in India hopes to build on past participatory work, although their direct 'clients' will be local women leaders. Similarly, the Asia Foundation initiative works with locally organised women and leaders. The South African development of economic literacy materials is intended to assist community-based groups in using the techniques and learning of gender budget analysis and advocacy.

A recently launched People's Budget process in South Africa raises questions about whether one will ever get broad-based support in using the approach of the Women's Budget Initiative. The new initiative is a collaborative effort of the Congress of South African Trade Unions, South African Council of Churches and South African NGO Coalition. The initiators have taken a conscious decision to focus on macro issues such as the basic income grant currently being considered by a government-appointed committee, land reform and debt. In proposing this strategy the key thinkers argue that focussing on these broad issues will facilitate widespread mobilisation and communication. They feel that the detailed attention paid to individual sectoral policies in the Women's Budget is not appropriate for their purposes. The argument makes sense to the extent that the organisers are contending that mass movements focus more easily on a few single issues. However, to be effective, this form of mobilisation needs a degree of mass support that the women's movement will not often enjoy. In addition, where poor women are concerned, one could well be more successful in mobilising around the 'small', sectoral everyday issues such as the details of education fees for their children, than around bigger, more 'public' issues.

Academics

The country studies indicate that some of the NGO initiatives draw on academics, particularly for research purposes. A few of the initiatives, such as the planned ones in Bangladesh and Italy, have academics at the forefront. NGOs have sometimes had difficulties, especially in the early years, in directing and overseeing the basic research. However, potential dangers of too great a separation of the role of advocate and researcher are that the advocates do not engage sufficiently with the content of the arguments or, alternatively, the researchers do not focus sufficiently on what is useful for practical advocacy purposes. Academic research usually allows for quite a lot of latitude in choosing the topic and shaping it to the readily available evidence and theory. Policy-advocated research, on the other hand, requires that the researcher stick to the topic no matter how difficult it is to find the necessary facts and theory. In Tanzania, TGNP has attempted to address some of these issues by having project teams made up of academics, NGO representatives and government officials.

In training, the use of academics can have both advantages and disadvantages. In some cases government officials respect academics more than NGO representatives. In others the academics are seen as impractical, theoretical and difficult to understand.

Individuals

If the above discussions seem to highlight in-country players in terms of institutions, it must be noted that individuals have also been extremely important in ensuring the achievements of the more successful initiatives. The Barbadian, Sri Lankan and Namibian cases point to the importance of having networks in key places in order to initiate the interventions. The Philippines example illustrates the importance of having gender activists scattered throughout the bureaucracy and in other powerful positions.

Ideally, however, GRB initiatives should not be reliant on the presence of individuals. The South African and Mozambiquan examples show what happens when key players disappear. The

Australian example, too, provides evidence of the importance of long-serving advocates in ensuring the survival of government initiatives. The challenge is to build up solid support and institutionalise initiatives while the climate is supportive so that they are less likely to be seen as 'disposable' when the climate changes.

Men

In Barbados, a man was the key player as project coordinator in the Ministry of Finance. This was particularly useful in a context where the notion of 'male marginalisation' is a common feature in discussions on gender issues. Men have, however, also played a role in many of the other GRB exercises. They have featured quite significantly as researchers, particularly in the African initiatives. Across countries men have also featured as the 'target group' for lobbying and training in government initiatives because of the dominant role they play in budgetary decision-making.

The Ugandan case study, however, raises the question of the extent to which men should be considered 'targets' in non-governmental initiatives. The Forum for Women in Democracy (FODOWE) argues that working with women separately is often better in order to build confidence and assertiveness.

Working at Different Levels of Government

Chile, Mexico, Peru, the Philippines, South Africa, Tanzania and Uganda are among the countries that have already initiated GRB work at the sub-national level. Projects planned for the future suggest that there will be more work at this level in the coming years.

Local level interventions are appropriate given that many countries – often under pressure from multilateral and bilateral institutions – are increasingly decentralising functions and budgets. Pragmatically, then, it makes sense to follow the money and decision-making power. So in Mexico, for example, Fundar and Equidad focus on the sub-national level, motivated by the shift in budget responsibility, particularly in social spending, to states and municipalities. They note that the decentralisation process has made 'controversial local budget decisions the centre of publicised political debates for the first time ever' (Fundar and Equidad de Genero, 1999:2).

The shift of focus to sub-national level should not be done unthinkingly. There may be a need to question decentralisation trends where, for example, this is accompanied by increasing inequality between the decentralised units or where functions are delegated but not money. Too often decentralisation can mean that the state is absolving itself of responsibilities, but attempting to do so in a way that is less visible. Often decentralisation will be justified by arguments that this promotes local 'ownership' and increases accountability whereas, in fact, local areas are simply being left to rely on their own meagre resources. So, for example, decentralisation is often accompanied by an increase in user fees for services. All of these aspects of decentralisation have gender implications. A local level focus needs to look at both what is happening in individual locations as well as the intergovernmental fiscal relations as a whole. The Third Women's Budget in South Africa provides one example of the latter aspect (De Bruyn and Budlender, 1998:50–88).

In Uganda, the Forum for Women in Democracy (FOWODE) argues that local level interventions are sensible in that poor women are unlikely, due to resource limitations, to be able to exert influence outside of this sphere. Interventions at this level may not, however, be easy. In many countries, traditional and potentially oppressive gender relations will often be more entrenched at local levels, while national leaders tend to be more aware of gender equity issues. The more blatant power relations – both in terms of gender and other factors – are directly reflected in local budgets in some countries. In the Philippines, for example, the Local Government Units' budgets usually contain a sizeable mayoral allocation over which the mayor has virtually complete discretion.

Where local government bodies are relatively small, the relationships between the key actors are often more direct and personal. The nature of these relationships needs to be taken into account in devising strategies. FOWODE's local initiative has engaged directly with the relationship issue by involving a wider range of players than at national level. So, for example, the first workshop brought together the mps elected in the districts, local councillors, local government officials and NGOs. One of the most heated debates during the training occurred when councillors' allowances were discussed.

Given the fluidity and changes in decentralised structures occurring in many countries, local level GRB initiatives which are directed at civil society or public representatives need to incorporate an explanation of the functions of different levels of government. This is important for advocacy purposes to prevent effort and resources being spent in lobbying those who have no power to address a particular problem. The differences across countries in the distribution of functions at different levels requires that special attention be paid to this when engaging in cross-country work.

Implementation Strategies

The term 'gender responsive budget' covers a number of distinctive activities or aims. In particular, it is used sometimes to refer to gendered analysis of budgets, and other times, to the creation of a gender-sensitive budget. Elson makes a slightly different distinction between the appraisal and planning stages of a budget, and the evaluation or auditing phases (personal communication). Logically, analysis of the budget must precede the creation of a gender-sensitive one, but there is also a difference in which of the activities different actors (typically government, parliamentarians and civil society) would focus on. Most of the strategies and techniques discussed in this section could be used for both analysis and actually making budgets.

Making an Impact on Expenditure Allocations and Revenue Measures

GRB exercises are not academic. They have the objective of influencing budget decision-making (Byanyima, 2000). As noted above, changing budget allocations is not their only objective. Nevertheless, it remains a central aim. Many of the initiatives can probably point to some changes in budget allocations for which they can claim partial credit. However, the impact on expenditure is usually limited.

A problem in terms of impact arises in the potential mismatch between allocations and expenditure. Those who engage in GRB analysis soon realise that allocations bear little resemblance to actual expenditures. Sometimes expenditure exceeds allocations. More often – and particularly in relation to gender responsive items – there is under-expenditure.

Sometimes the under-expenditure reflects outright lack of concern about gender or other important issues. More often the under-expenditure reflects deeper problems in the budgeting or other systems, such as limited revenues (many countries!), cash budgeting (Tanzania), delayed sanctioning of expenditure (India) or unforeseen expenditures on wars, natural disasters or debt repayments (Mozambique). The poverty alleviation funds in South Africa provide an example where under-expenditure can be partly explained by insufficient attention having been paid to how the allocations were to be managed and implemented.

An examination of actual expenditure can capture this problem of under-expenditure in asking how much was spent and on what. Unfortunately, in many countries this information is not readily available or is only available in subsequent budget years. The problem can then be written off as an historical one, whereas problems reported sooner could more easily result in corrective action. Few GRB initiatives to date have paid much attention to the discrepancies between allocations and expenditure. One suggested way of tackling the problem is to identify services which do reach (poor) people and then identify, service by service, the relevance of the services in meeting women's needs and the costs borne in obtaining them (Goetz, 1995). The gender budget audit referred to below also promises opportunities.

Research

Research can play an important role in GRB initiatives. Firstly, knowledge of technical 'facts and figures' can make those in power take arguments about gender seriously, rather than dismissing them as simply emotive or moral issues. Secondly, knowledge of the facts and figures can give gender advocates the confidence required to push forward with their arguments rather than be intimidated. Thirdly, a large part of what is referred to as 'research' in the GRB initiatives could more accurately be described as finding out how systems work. In particular, it is about how decision making around policy and budget functions and where it could be useful to intervene.

One important difference between budget research and some other research is the importance of timing. So, for example, both the South African and Ugandan initiatives timed the dissemination of their research to coincide with the day on which the national budget was presented. In both cases, the organisers were aware that at this stage there was little hope of changing any budget figures. However, they also knew that research released at this time would be more likely to get the attention of parliamentarians, who could utilise it in their budget speeches, and of the media. Information is crucial to any successful advocacy strategy.

Most GRB analysts bemoan the paucity of information, particularly of gender-disaggregated data. The reasons for these problems include the format of most budget documents and a high degree of aggregation of figures. Goetz (1994) suggests that policy makers often overstate the lack of gender-disaggregated information to explain the absence of gender equity policies or programmes. Krug and van Staveren note that the official auditing institutions are usually also affected, as it is the bureaucrats who supply the auditing institutions with data. They refer to this particular problem as 'asymmetric information' or 'selective inattentiveness'. In such a situation, independent research can be important in placing the information in front of those who do not 'want to know'. Even limited information can often be sufficient to illuminate important points for advocacy and to start mobilisation.

Simkins (1999), discussing non-gender-specific policy work, points to the opposite problem: one of having too much data. This is particularly acute when the bulk of available data is not organised in a form that is useful for analytical purposes. This second problem has presented a challenge in several of the

existing initiatives where the budget documents are large, old-style computer-formatted lists of numbers under unclear headings. The problem is exacerbated when one discovers computation and other errors among the many numbers. The move towards output, performance or programme budgeting in various countries suggests that an over-abundance of information may soon become a more common problem.

One tension with research is how to reach sufficient sophistication to be able to convince and argue with technicians, while keeping it simple enough to be understood by less educated or less technical gender advocates. Some of these 'popular' versions of materials have being criticised for being 'condescending'. However, parliamentarians and others have often utilised these materials to a greater extent than the 'more substantial' versions for reasons of brevity and convenience. South Africa has produced separate materials with simplified language and concepts for advocacy and training, such as Money Matters. Programmes in Tanzania and Uganda have also produced shorter and 'popular' versions of their materials. Uganda has also supplemented this with short issue briefs for parliamentarians that focus on key issues.

A research challenge is that most people feel intimidated when they embark on gender responsive budget analysis as the field is new and there are no set recipes. However, when the research is complete, these same researchers generally feel a sense of real achievement. For planning purposes, this means that a mechanism for support and encouragement should be built into the process.

Another potential problem is that the research and fact-based empirical approach that underlies most GRB initiatives often assumes that policy and budgets, and related changes, are based on rational analysis. Yet a study which looks at the largely US-based literature on the utilisation of social science research in policy making argues that this is seldom the case (Glover, 1993). Generally, it is probably true that research which supports a popular option will be listened to, but that which opposes it will be ignored. Stated more bluntly, it is politics and power than determine policy more than anything else. Further, Glover also argues that policy makers tend to emphasise distributional

concerns, 'to assess costs and benefits in terms of the number of people affected, rather than financial costs and benefits [while] economists emphasise efficiency'. This begs the question, with respect to budget policy, as to what happens when economists predominate among the policy makers.

Analytical Tools

From the outset, one of the aims of the Commonwealth Secretariat initiative was to create a set of analytical tools for budgetary expenditure analysis that could be used by different governments. Diane Elson did important conceptual work in delineating six broad categories of tools:[1]

- Gender-Aware Policy Appraisal
- Beneficiary Assessments
- Public Expenditure Incidence Analysis
- Gender-Disaggregated Analysis of the Budget on Time Use
- Gender-Aware Medium-Term Economic Policy Framework
- Gender Responsive Budget Statement.

The first four were intended for testing in the pilot countries, and the country profiles in the next section give examples of the use of all four, although to varying extents and with different understandings as to what they mean. The last two were seen as requiring further development and data before they could be implemented. The Commonwealth Secretariat and AusAID also commissioned the development of a training manual based on the application of these tools in country-level programme implementation (Budlender and Sharp, 1998). In practice, while the list of Elson tools is widely quoted, the step to implementation is not easy and the demand for tools continues.

Simel Esim (1995), in an early paper for the World Bank, categorises the different methods of analysing expenditure as follows:

---

1 See Annex to the Elson article.

- Classical Economic Analysis:
  - Evaluation of public expenditures – aggregate level, composition of goods government needs to provide
  - Evaluation of functional composition of expenditures – inter- or intra-sectoral
  - Evaluation of economic composition within and across sectors – capital, current, wages and other
- Institutional analysis – improving ability to make effective use of resources
- Analysis of delivery mechanisms – including alternatives to government provision
- Analysis of quality of services
- Stakeholder analysis – explores opportunities and impediments
- Public expenditure incidence analysis – depends on allocation of spending and household behaviour
- Qualitative methods
  - Beneficiary assessment
  - Participatory Poverty Assessment

The list is useful in showing the number of potential methods. However, as it stands it does not explain when and how these methods need to be adapted so as to provide gender-sensitive analysis. For example, simple beneficiary incidence analysis (public expenditure incidence analysis) provides a partial view if it does not incorporate some measure of the differential need of women and men, girls and boys rather than simply who is reached.

In Tanzania TGNP responded to the demand for tools by developing a checklist that planners and budget officers can use alongside the other manuals in ensuring gender main-streaming. But the Commonwealth/AUSAID manual at several points stresses that the notion of 'tools' should not be understood mechanically. In particular, it stresses that gender analysis itself is probably the most important tool for gender mainstreaming.

Analytical Frameworks

There are a number of basic frameworks, which, with variations, have served as the basis of many exercises to date. These include: 1. Rhonda Sharp's three-way categorisation of expenditure; 2. the South African four or five step approach; and 3. the Australian-type format proposed in the Commonwealth/AUSAID manual.

1. The three-way categorisation distinguishes between (a) gender-targeted expenditure; (b) equal opportunity expenditure for civil servants; and (c) mainstream expenditure (the rest) considered in terms of its gendered impact (the Elson article has a pictorial representation). The classification is based on that used for the South Australian Women's Budget when it was framed in terms of 'women' rather than 'gender'. The classification has proved useful in pointing out that a focus on the limited funds usually allocated to category (a) misses the point of the exercise. It has also proved useful when working with government officials, in highlighting the need to move from a focus on opportunities for women civil servants (category b) to how government expenditure delivers to the general public.

One weakness of this framework is the confusion between women and gender. In particular, expenditures that are targeted at women may not necessarily advance gender equity. For example, family planning expenditures that focus only on population control through control of women's bodies would usually not be regarded as gender-sensitive. A second weakness is that the framework only applies to expenditure, while a parallel framework for revenue has not proved as popular. This may be because of lesser attention to revenue but perhaps also because of the vast differences in revenue issues between developed and developing countries.

2. The four- or five-step approach is the situation analysis, policy, budget, and implementation method described above (under civil society). The number of steps expands to five if one distinguishes between short-term outputs of expenditure (or revenue) and longer-term outcomes. This framework forms the basis of the policy appraisal that is one of Elson's six tools. It is also very similar to the inputs, activities, outputs and impacts

framework, which she has used in her more recent work. The framework has been used for outside-government initiatives such as those of South Africa, Tanzania and Uganda. It has been used more often for expenditure than revenue but can be easily adapted for the latter.

In practice, the main weakness in the use of this approach has been a limited ability to move beyond the second step. Generally the researchers involved are practised in describing the situation and discussing policy, but the sections on budget are brief and often weak. The blame does not always lie with the researchers. Often the necessary data are simply not available.

However, in many cases the facts are there for those who look. While many complain that budgets tell very little, even the simplest tables sometimes expose serious imbalances. The documents that accompany the budget figures can also be revealing. The quote below is an extract from a local government budget speech. The contradiction between the concern with the poorest and a first priority that involves transport for councillors and officials will be clear to most readers without sophisticated analysis:

'During this year we shall strive to ensure that our people and in particular the poorest members of our community benefit from council's development initiatives. To ensure that this happens council intends to focus its spending on three objectives:

Strengthening Public Administration and other good governance institutions ... In relation with this important aspect funds are being provided in this budget to enable Honourable members of council to be facilitated to acquire reasonable means of transport to help them with mobilization in their constituencies. In the same vein Honourable members will this afternoon be requested to approve a Co-ownership Scheme that will enable 5 Secretaries of the District Executive Committee to pay back to council 40% of the net cost of their motorcycles and thereafter own them ...'

3. The Commonwealth approach was designed for training of civil servants. It is similar to the step model, but more tightly specified. The standard format is suitable for the bureaucratic environment. One weakness of the method is that it can be boring for both the compiler and the reader if it is applied

across all programmes and policies. Yet it is precisely this comprehensiveness that is necessary in a full audit. Another weakness is again the absence of data. But because the method is used largely in government, exposing these gaps has a greater chance of generating corrective action. The Sri Lankan exercise, where sectoral officials initiated special surveys to collect the necessary gender-disaggregated data, is very encouraging here.

The distinction between the third, more formal method and the two looser, more experimental ones is presented above as matching the government-NGO divide (governments should use the more formal method and NGOs the looser one). In South Africa we have explicitly argued that the two groupings have different roles to play in terms of gender responsive budgets. We see governments using GRB techniques for internal management purposes and for reporting and accountability purposes to parliament and the public. We see civil society and parliament using GRB techniques to hold government to account. We argue that civil society is more suited for the methodological experimentation that is still necessary to uncover the many implicit and hidden ways in which gender bias occurs.

Besides the standard approaches, there are several welcome examples of experimentation with various types of modelling. For example, Joseph Tumushabe (forthcoming) has modelled the costs and savings that a series of educational reforms could introduce in the education budget of Uganda. In Malawi, Naomi Ngwira is attempting to link macroeconomic policy analysis and gender responsive budgets through a gender financing gap model. Modelling exercises are unlikely to reach a wide audience, but are important in developing the sophistication of analysis.

Understanding Budgetary Process and Procedures

Several of the GRB exercises have focused some attention away from budgetary policy, programmes and allocations onto the budget process itself. This is especially common in exercises outside-of-government. Most descriptions document the paucity of women among the top decision-makers. But they also go further in describing the key actors, their respective roles and at which stage they participate.

An understanding of the budget process allows activists to determine where and when to place their efforts so as to have the greatest likelihood of success, i.e. it helps identify the 'strategic entry points'. Understanding of the process is also important for training and implementation purposes, in terms of where and in what way particular groups of stakeholders and participants can have an impact and should be involved in the initiative. Too often, the responses in evaluations of workshops include a complaint that the key groups have been omitted from the training.

In any country's budget process, there are usually multiple decision-making points and players. Some are formally acknowledged and visible, while others are informal and not easily recognised. For example, during research in South Africa into a local government budget, the researchers were informed that the draft budget was routinely discussed with the chamber of commerce before presentation to the council. Yet this was not part of the formally documented process. In a local government workshop in Uganda, a somewhat similar phenomenon was found. Participants from four districts were asked to describe the budget process in their area. Each of them included in the description preliminary discussions with the community about their needs. Yet this step is not included in the official guidelines of the central Ministry of Financial Planning and Economic Development.

Examining only the formal procedures may fail to indicate who really has power, or which actors are fully participants as opposed to those who are involved simply as a formality. One advantage of involving a wide range of stakeholders in GRB initiatives is that within this multiplicity there are likely to be some who engage meaningfully with and can speak about, rather than speculate on, the actual budgetary processes and powers.

At the micro-level, attention to process will often reveal a disjuncture between those responsible for the different steps implicit in developing and implementing budgets, that is, situation analysis, policy, budgets, implementation and auditing. For example, it could be the information systems people who are responsible for situation analysis, planners for making policy, budget officers for budgets, fieldworkers for implementation and an internal or external accounting group for auditing. Here it is not only a question of whom to lobby to get change, but also of getting the different groups to communicate with each other. Workshops bringing them together are one step in this direction. However, these are unlikely, without a lot of further effort, to ensure that the different groups continue to work across their bureaucratic and functional boundaries.

In stable situations planning and budgeting processes become routine processes that change little from year to year. This very stability can lead to an inertia that sometimes makes any changes very difficult. Fluid situations offer greater opportunities for innovation, but also a strong possibility that the next round of inevitable reforms will negate any progress made.

In South Africa there are at least two instances where gender innovations in fiscal policy were overridden by subsequent changes in the process. At the national level, the gender-related discussions introduced during the Commonwealth Secretariat gender responsive budget initiative do not fit as easily into the new format budget to be used for 2001/2 as they did previously. At the provincial level, one of the reasons that detailed work by departments on engendering the 'key measurable objectives' diminished in the subsequent fiscal policy document was the change in authority structures under the new Public Finance Management Act. A second reason was the failure to achieve sufficient consensus among all the necessary top policy-makers that gender responsive budgets were important.

Training

Virtually all initiatives include some element of training or capacity building. This includes training for researchers, for different types of advocates and for government officials. Types of advocates can include public representatives such as MPs and local councillors, NGOs and other civil society activists. In a Ugandan workshop, a Ministry of Finance official also argued strongly that she, herself, was an internal advocate. Many officials from Gender Affairs Ministries would support this view.

In terms of subject matter, there are big variations in training programmes. Most GRB workshops will devote some time to awareness raising in respect of gender. Those directed at civil society will probably devote some time to advocacy and lobbying skills. Workshops for researchers and bureaucrats will probably concentrate more on technical skills. However, if they are to be effective, they will also need to include awareness raising and some discussion of power and decision-making. South Africa's workshop materials attempt to cater for different needs by adopting a modular approach where workshop designers can choose which inputs and exercises are appropriate for different audiences.

Many of the workshop facilitators come from outside government. This poses special challenges when running workshops for government officials, many of whom may be wary as to what those outside can teach them, in addition to being suspicious about motives. A report on a training initiative on gender and macroeconomics which brought together economic planning ministries and women's bureaux notes the need to validate the skills and expertise of participants so as to allow them to learn from each other (Pearson, 1995). Sen (1999) makes a similar point in relation to training for Ministry of Finance officials. We can extend these two observations and state that in any workshop there should (a) be respect for and acknowledgement of the knowledge participants bring and (b) the opportunity for participants and facilitators to learn from each other.

Cross-country Work

In cross-country work there is always a tension around whether to use examples from countries other than the one you are working in. The tension is particularly acute in respect of work on gender. Firstly, there is the possibility that the examples can be dismissed on the grounds that gender is a 'cultural' issue that is country-specific. As a (white) resident of the dominant country in the Southern African region, I am very aware of possible resistance to over-use of South African experts and

South African examples. There would probably be similar tensions in other regions in respect of specific countries. Secondly, where participants have difficulties in understanding their own budgets, adding examples with different formats, structures and context increases the complexity.

On the other hand, examples from other countries allow distance, which can make participants less defensive and thus more critical in their observations. Exercises such as the comparison of the South African government and civil society views on community care seem to work well across countries with very minor changes. They can also open eyes to what might seem inconceivable possibilities. Certainly, South Africa's constitutional provision in respect of non-discrimination in terms of sexual preference, Barbados' VAT-exemption for cocoa, Tanzania's breastfeeding leave of two hours a day, and Uganda's university admission policy whereby young women need fewer marks than men, always help people to recognise that the boundaries can be pushed quite far.

Language is also an issue since at this stage most of the material on gender responsive budgets is in English. Even at the non-popular level, there is limited material available in other languages, including those used across many countries, such as Spanish.

Adding the Time Dimension

Reproductive work, or the care economy, is a central concept in most GRB work. It is often mentioned in reports and analyses. Yet the Swiss study is one of the few to attempt serious quantification of the budget's impact on reproductive work. Even here, those responsible acknowledged that this aspect of their work was the one that needed the most development if it was to be taken seriously.

Time use studies can provide important base data for taking this type of analysis forward. Until recently, there were very few time use studies in developing countries. However, between 1995 and 2000 there were dedicated or modular-type time use studies in over twenty: Benin, Chad, Cuba (pilot), Guatemala, Honduras, Ecuador, Dominican Republic, India (very large pilot), Indonesia (pilot), South Korea, Lao People's Democratic Republic, Mexico, Mongolia, Morocco, Nepal, Nicaragua, Nigeria, Oman, Palestine, Philippines (pilot), South Africa and Vietnam. Thus far, though, the data has not been used in GRB initiatives.

Grown *et al.* (2000) suggest that there are four ways in which gender can be incorporated into macroeconomic modelling. Goetz (1995) suggests, in particular, that gender-sensitive social accounting matrices (SAMs) could be used to measure the impact of fiscal policy. Gender can be relatively easily incorporated into SAMs on the factor side as most countries have gender-disaggregated information about (paid) labour. A more exciting possibility is to add flows of unpaid labour into the models. Again, this is an area in which there is little work at present, although some is planned in the near future. The January 2000 regional UNIFEM workshop in Cuba focused on household and time use surveys as well as national budgets and has, hopefully, stimulated interest in that region.

Gender and Women

Virtually all presentations of the South African Women's Budget Initiative provoke a question from the audience as to why the name includes the word 'women' rather than 'gender'. While the simple answer might be that it copied the Australians, a more thoughtful response is that the unashamed use of the word 'women' is reflected elsewhere in South Africa, for example in the naming of many parts of the state's gender machinery. Most of the people inside this machinery would, nevertheless, support 'gender analysis' and a GAD rather than wid framework. The choice of 'women' partly reflects an emphasis on the empowerment of women, and partly an understanding of gender relations that sees women, in most cases, being the ones adversely affected by gender bias.

The women-gender issue is not confined to South Africa. In many of the GRB initiatives there is slippage between the use of 'women' and 'gender'. In some cases the slippage is unconscious. In others it is intentional, in that those responsible are trying to build a broader base of people who promote GRB work.

Many gender analysts may balk at this cautious approach and it can also easily lead to projects and programmes that are sub-optimal in terms of promoting gender equity, or which even reinforce inequalities. Nevertheless, the pragmatism of the careful approach might in some cases prove more sustainable than a 'purer' stance.

Use of the word 'gender' does not, in itself, guarantee that there is gender analysis. In many initiatives there are frequent references to 'women and poor men', or 'women and poor people'. In Uganda, people with disabilities are often appended, reflecting their presence in the parliamentary interest group caucus. The 'poor men/people' approach emphasises economic disadvantage, which is certainly important. However, the phrase could be taken to suggest that all women are poor or that all women are equally disadvantaged. More nuanced analysis would distinguish between different types of women in different positions. These differences influence their needs and the extent to which they should be a priority for government intervention.

The South African initiative, because of our apartheid past, is particularly insistent on distinguishing between black and white women and between those who live in the former rural 'homelands' and those who live in former 'white' South Africa. In some other initiatives, there is scope for paying more attention to the different roles, needs and interests of different categories of women. In the Caribbean context, the Barbados report notes that a focus on gender 'is often taken to mean that men will be included where they have been neglected in development strategy and public policy' (St Hill, 2000:4).

Equity or Efficiency

Goetz notes that efficiency arguments are powerful in developing countries, given the emphasis most agencies place on modernisation and increasing productivity. However, she also notes the dangers of too heavy a focus on efficiency. Firstly, she asks what one then does when there is counter-evidence that suggests that measures that promote gender equality have a cost. Secondly, she argues that 'the productivist paradigm ...

does not challenge the ideologies and practices of development bureaucracies. It conforms to a utilitarian penchant for measuring worth, or 'equality', in terms of money or a close substitute' (Goetz, 1994:32).

The United Kingdom country profile notes the Women Budget Group's use of efficiency arguments rather than arguments of equity. But it also notes that the Group stresses that 'efficiency' needs to be broadened beyond the traditional economic meaning. This approach addresses the second point raised by Goetz.

While there are dangers in focusing too much on efficiency, equity arguments also have their weaknesses. In particular, arguments based on the fact that a particular country has signed the Convention on the Elimination of All Forms of Discrimination Against Women (CEDAW), or some other international or national instrument, usually carries more weight with gender advocates than those in top decision-making positions. Pragmatically, one can say that both types of argument can be useful in the right place and for the right audience. Both are 'tools'

Gender Audits

The Australian country profile notes that New South Wales moved 'beyond' gender responsive budgets to gender audits. In this case, the term gender audit was used to indicate that the assessment included more than budgets. However, terms are used in different ways. Firstly, most GRB initiatives look at more than budgets; and secondly, some commentators, such as Krug and van Staveren, use the term 'gender audit' explicitly to refer to the scrutiny of government budgets (1999).

Right within budget work there is an explicit audit function. In most countries the main responsibility for auditing the budget will be vested in an agency separate from the Ministry of Finance. There has been little gender work in the auditing agencies to date. However, there is a relatively new regional initiative in South-East Africa, driven by Kenya and funded by SIDA, which has conducted a number of workshops. Officials of the Tanzanian Office of the Controller and Auditor-General have also recently completed materials.

Links to other Developmental Programmes

While often inspired by broader global and macroeconomic developments such as structural adjustment programmes and levels of indebtedness, most gender responsive budgets have focused more on sectoral level impacts. However, either implicitly or explicitly, many of the initiatives are targeted at the wider or 'big' issues and their impacts. For example, the most popular choices of focus, education and health, reflect the fact that the social sectors were often constrained by structural adjustment programmes. Similarly, within the focus on agriculture, initiatives usually discuss the gendered impact of the focus on modernisation, commercialisation and globalisation rather than subsistence production.

Debt and Poverty

In Uganda and Tanzania there have been links between the GRB initiatives and the highly indebted poor country initiative (HIPC) processes. In Uganda in late 1999, the Uganda Debt Network, as the central NGO player on the debt issue, together with the Asia Foundation's Global Women in Politics Programme, organised a workshop on budgets and gender. The Network has focused its attention on the special poverty-related allocations that HIPC releases and participates in government forums on this issue. The newly constituted Poverty Working Group identified 'specific concerns of women' as one of the five themes to be investigated through quantitative and participatory analysis in preparation for the 2000 budget process (McGee, 2000:43). At the GRB workshop, the Network expressed interest in maintaining contact and stimulating interest in budget work by other organisations. To date, it seems that FOWODE, which participated in the workshop, has continued to be the main actor in respect of gender responsive budgets. In its work FOWODE has chosen to focus on the budget as a whole rather than the HIPC related allocations.

In Tanzania, both the government and TGNP are keen to ensure that budgets reflect the priorities stipulated in the Poverty Reduction Strategy Paper (PRSP) and other macro policy frameworks. TGNP participated in the PRSP process but was not happy with either the process or results. One problem is that the PRSP logical framework has not carried through the gendered analysis reflected in the discursive parts of the document.

The World Bank specifies that public participation is a prerequisite for acceptance of the strategy papers. However, there is some scepticism among observers as to how genuine the Bank's interest in participation is. A World Vision booklet notes that 'although proclaimed as a new degree of local control and poverty focus, the PRSPs could be seen by critics as no more than a route to buy off criticism for the Bank and the IMF. They are therefore, potentially more suited to meeting the needs of global institutions than to serving the needs of the poor' (quoted in Bretton Woods Update, December 2000). In Tanzania, the consultants responsible for the final PRSP document responded to the criticism of gender advocates with the argument that there was not sufficient time to mainstream gender in the logframe as they needed to meet the IMF and World Bank deadlines. They suggested that the strategy was a multi-year one and that there would therefore be room for amendments as it progressed. Despite the problems, the PRSP process could offer an opening for strong groups in countries with progressive governments. In Tanzania, after lobbying, the PRSP drafters agreed to a special meeting with gender advocates.

Public Expenditure Reviews

Another potential area for intervention is the public expenditure reviews (PERs). The World Bank coordinates about 25 of these country-level reviews each year. Usually bilateral donors are also involved. In many countries governments have been unhappy with how these reviews have been conducted in the past, seeing them as judgements and impositions by the multilateral and bilateral agencies more than anything else. Elson and Cagatay suggest that the purpose of the reviews is more to impose fiscal restraint or efficiency than about eradicating poverty (1999: 10). In recent years governments of countries such as Vietnam and Tanzania have attempted to take more control of the exercises. In Vietnam there was an attempt to incorporate gender within the review but, as noted in the case study, the result was limited by inadequate conceptualisation of what this would mean on the part of the Bank. In Tanzania, TGNP has participated in the PER meetings but has been less directly involved in the core analyses.

Medium-Term Expenditure Frameworks

The country profiles indicate that Ireland is attempting to incorporate a gender perspective into its National Development Plan, which is a multi-year expenditure plan. Many developing countries are also currently moving to multi-year budgets. These could provide opportunities, particularly as gender equality is a longer-term goal that cannot be achieved in a single year.

For those in authority there may be other reasons for introducing multi-year budgets than allowing broader input into development goals and direction. The South African Department of Finance explains that the main benefits of medium-term budgeting are as follows (Department of Finance, 1998: 1):

- 'enabling spending agencies to consider how best to deliver public services and transformation within realistic projections of their budgets;
- establishing a framework for assessing new policy proposals;
- fostering medium-term planning by spending agencies;
- allowing agencies to enter into forward commitments without requiring rollovers of unspent prior allocations; and
- improving the credibility of fiscal policy'.

What is noteworthy is that this description has no mention of participation by parliament or civil society.

Output and Performance Budgeting

The introduction of medium-term expenditure frameworks often goes hand in hand with the introduction of output, programme or performance type budgeting systems. Here, again, it seems there might be possibilities for gender advocates in that each of these budgeting systems introduces indicators that should measure concrete delivery. In the case studies, this point is noted, historically, for Australia and as a future potential for Switzerland. The South African and Tanzanian government initiatives are among those that have focused on developing gender-sensitive indicators.

Again, there are challenges. The introduction of indicators is often motivated by a desire to make officials accountable in terms of new forms of performance contracts. This form of accountability does not necessarily include accountability to citizens or even parliaments. Further, the standard way of approaching indicators is to argue that they must measure the three 'E's – efficiency, economy and effectiveness. With the exception of Tasmania, the ministries appear to forget the fourth 'E' – equity.

Forward to Sustainability

This overview and the country profiles in the next section give some idea of the diversity of activities that have taken place under the guise of 'gender responsive budgets'. However, these do not cover either all the possible considerations, or all the complexities of each individual consideration. The situation is complicated by the fact that the Commonwealth Secretariat, IDRC and UNIFEM will rarely, because of the necessity of country ownership, be initiating action in the absence of recognised in-country capacity and commitment. Their preferred role will be to support initiatives planned and undertaken by others. Bearing this in mind, the following presents some suggestions as to principles that the programme might embrace in moving forward. It also provides a checklist that could be used as a starting point in evaluating requests for assistance, and in evaluating what initiatives have achieved at the end of the support programme.

The Triangle of Players

The Asia Foundation's GRB work is based on the idea that gender responsive budgets that focus on good governance involve 'the informed participation of three interconnected sets of stakeholders – progressive elected officials at the national and local levels; effective government institutions staffed with technically qualified individuals; and active, well-informed coalitions of NGOs and people's organisations capable of articulating demands based on felt material needs and basic human rights' (quoted in Carr, 2000). This formulation serves to emphasise that, in any single country, there are many different players to address and many ingredients that are necessary for GRB initiatives. Any single project will probably not be able to tackle all these components, but each project should be aware of what is happening in each corner of the potential triangle.

Claim Victories but Admit Weaknesses

GRB initiatives need both to claim victories and acknowledge weaknesses. Both aspects are important if the initiatives are to learn from each other. For every country profile included, there would be another possible rendering which could portray it as much less or much more successful. All the initiatives have their weaknesses and there is not a single country in the world that can claim that their budget is totally gender responsive. However it is too easy to be cynical, and this can lead to abandoning any attempts at intervention.

One of the objectives of gender responsive budgets is to get people – and especially women – involved and doing things. This is an objective in itself. Similarly, changing the outlook of civil servants and other people in positions of power may not be immediately visible in budget and policy terms, but can facilitate later changes. Further, preventing 'bad' changes in budget lines, while less visible than adding 'good' lines, is often as difficult to achieve in a context where there are strong forces working against gender equity and social-responsive programmes and expenditures.

Overall, then, building partnerships between governments and civil society and other process-related outcomes can be as important a result as changing budget lines, although less easily measurable. As Blair (2001: vii) notes in respect of US support for civil society participation, it perhaps makes 'sense to say that success occurs when civil society organisations were able to make the discourse robust enough, and the media coverage vigorous enough that decision-making was reasonably transparent'. Only then will the 'major stakeholders feel they have been taken seriously, and (most important) will they stay in the game'.

Learning From Others

While often heavily influenced by international financial institutions, ultimately budgets are devised and implemented at the country-level. This must influence the planning of gender responsive budgets as, for the most part, the activity will need to focus on one country at a time. Regional or broader inter-country initiatives might be useful in raising awareness and strengthening capacity, particularly where countries have similar socio-economic and gender situations, and similar forms and processes of budgeting and governance. Further, examples from elsewhere have sometimes inspired initiatives in countries very far from the original country. However, in practice it is usually the copying of an idea rather than the format or approach. So, for example, while South Africa and Philippines both say they borrowed the idea from Australia, they are very different both from each other and from Australia (see country profiles). Ultimately, the initiative has to be fought out on the country terrain.

No Micro-Management

Gender responsive budgets are difficult to plan. Firstly, they are still experimental. Secondly, and more importantly, they operate in an intensely political arena. If logical framework planning is used, the 'assumptions' column will be fuller than usual. If we compare what was planned with what was actually achieved in country initiatives to date, there would almost certainly be variances – some positive, some negative.

Most external agencies are aware that their programme will not be successful if they micro-manage what happens in different countries. Indeed, this would go against the ethos of a project that is also about (self) governance and democracy. On the other hand, agencies which provide support will of course need to have sufficient planning and reporting from those they are assisting to ensure that the project itself is accountable and is implemented well. That balance will not be easy to establish but is important to maintain.

Tempering the Search for Universal Tools

Porter and Smyth observe that experience has shown that the search for universal frameworks and tools for doing gender-sensitive work was somewhat misguided (1999: 329). Elson, too, suggests that there is no 'blueprint' in terms of tools for GRB analysis (Senapaty, 2000: 6). This point could be made even more strongly if we talk about tools for GRB work as a whole, rather than only analysis. That said, GRB training, especially when directed at government officials, needs to move beyond gender sensitisation to provide the officials with clear guidelines as to how to give effect to their new-found sensitivity in their job.

Training with a Purpose

Given the current popularity of GRB initiatives internationally, there may be a tendency among multi-and bilateral agencies or country-level stakeholders to want to organise training workshops. However, this ambition needs to be linked to a concrete situation if the outcomes of the training are to be meaningful. Experience has shown that where training has been organised without careful consideration of the purpose and the target group and a clear sense of follow-up, it has proven to be of limited value for the organisers and participants. Given the scarce resources available to support gender and other developmental programmes, clarity on the objectives of all planned activities is imperative.

What constitutes an initiative?

Gender budgets are a tool. They are not an end in themselves. The country profiles largely reflect stand-alone initiatives where the focus is firmly on gender budgets. But gender budget analysis or advocacy can also be part of other initiatives and, ideally, should be if mainstreaming is a serious objective. The Commonwealth Secretariat GRB project will need to decide whether it will provide support only to focused initiatives, or rather be open to the possibility of providing support to cases where gender budget work is part of a larger project.

Seizing the Moment

Several of the case studies suggest that GRB initiatives have most chance of success in situations of change, for example, when there is a new government or a shift in policy. As noted, in most countries budgets are rather stable instruments with minor changes from year to year. Where there are political, policy or other shifts, government officials might be more disposed to taking on board new ideas, and advocates might be more excited about working on issues. Many changes are not predictable, so planning interventions on this basis is not always possible. Strategically, though, a focus on change might help in selecting countries for intervention, as well as selecting what issues to focus on within countries.

Building Linkages

GRB initiatives are strengthened when they make linkages. To date the extent to which this work has been taken up by 'general' or 'mainstream' stakeholders varies from country to country. For example, the International Budget Project, which is an international think-tank promoting budget reform, generally refers to the gender components in a few paragraphs or a case study rather than seeing it as integral to other budget work. Yet the number of times that gender or women are mentioned in the case studies suggests that there are a range of groups that would be interested in more focused GRB work.

A similar point can be made about the Alternative Federal Budget process in Canada. Publications such as 'A Taste of Success' (The International Budget Project, 2000) or 'Show Us the Money' (Loxley, 2000) also have rich experiences that GRB initiatives could draw on in terms of approaches and strategies. Similarly, the links with other advocates for transparency, accountability, and public participation are often not as strong as they should or could be. The lack of linkages lessens the impact of GRB work, and lessens the effectiveness and equity of non-gender-specific work..

Driving an Initiative

None of the many initiatives described in the country profiles appear to have anyone working full-time on them. Further, in each of the projects there are probably only one or two people who see themselves as centrally responsible for the work. While appropriate for arranging a one-off workshop or conference, this limited human resource configuration does not lend itself easily to sustaining longer-term work. The latter requires ongoing commitment from the key stakeholders, and a capacity to research, coordinate, inform and to motivate, nag, nudge and drag other players to commit time to a GRB exercise when they are being pulled in many other directions. This will need to be considered in planning institutional arrangements for initiatives.

This is Politics

Gender responsive budgets are political. While many components of the work, or indeed of budget work more generally, are technical, the discussion above points to ways in which this technicality obscures crucial political and ideological positions. Further, even within a particular framework, technical knowledge alone will not produce significant change or sustainable results. The project needs to think through all the implications of the political economy of the exercises. These include the choice of actors, how to work with or around key decision-makers, how to present the work to different groups and the arguments, where and how to build in advocacy, and so on.

A Checklist

The checklist below is intended as a guide in determining the nature of a particular initiative. The items on the list below are not intended to have a judging function, i.e. one particular answer to any of the questions is not intrinsically 'better' than another.

- Who are the key drivers in the initiative? Are they in government, parliament, or civil society?
- What links do the key drivers have with other players? Have they worked together on other projects? Do government and the outside government players regard themselves as allies or in opposition?
- If government is involved, which agencies – Ministry of Finance, Planning, Statistics, gender machinery, delivery agencies?
- If civil society is involved, what type of organisations – women's organisations, mixed organisations, sectoral organisations, research and policy groups, academics?
- Which level of government does the initiative focus on – national or sub-national? If sub-national, how are sub-regions chosen?
- Which aspects of the budget does the initiative focus on – expenditure or revenue?
- Which parts of the policy-making process is the initiative targeting – planning, implementation, monitoring and evaluation?
- What activities are planned – research, publication, materials development, advocacy, training?
- Who is the 'audience' for the initiative?
- What expertise do the key drivers have in terms of discipline, experience in public administration, research, training, materials production, advocacy?
- What previous work has been done by the initiating group and others on budget analysis?
- What previous work has been done by the initiating group and others in the field of gender?
- What are the other important axes of disadvantage, in addition to gender, in the country? To what extent does the initiative address these?

- What is the government stance, policy and record in respect of gender?
- What are the key policy and development-related activities in the country at present, and how – if at all – does the initiative link up with these?
- What is the overall political situation in terms of political stability or change, levels and processes of political participation, and progressive or otherwise orientation of government?
- Who currently participates in the budget process in the country?
- How transparent is government – how easy is it to obtain information about budgets and related issues?
- What roles do the multilateral and bilateral agencies play in determining policies and budgets in the country? What roles will these agencies play in the initiative?

Final Words

Work on gender responsive budgets can and should be both immensely satisfying and fun.

A Profile of Country Activities

Debbie Budlender

When writing these country profiles, I endeavoured to contact people involved in all the initiatives I heard or read about. If the report contains errors of fact or errors of judgement, I apologise for these. Many thanks to Alcinda Abreu, Haroon Akram-Lodhi, Pat Alailima, Melanie Beresford, Letty Chiwara, Lorraine Corner, Diane Elson, Simel Esim, Barbara Evers, Regina Frey, Pregs Govender, Marge Guerrero, Guy Hewitt, Sue Himmelweit, Helena Hofbauer, Kareen Jabre, Wanjiku Kabira, Joanna Kerr, Jennifer Klot, Ann Lehman, Mascha Madorin, Gabriele Michalitsch, Rebecca Pearl, Mary Rusimbi, Donna St. Hill, Manju Senapaty, Elizabeth Stiefel, Rhonda Sharp, Shirin Shukri and Kaniz Siddique for the invaluable information they provided.

Introduction

The methodology used to prepare these country profiles was primarily a desk review. The review included both official and unofficial documents collected during a lengthy involvement in the area, as well as documents provided by the Commonwealth Secretariat and UNIFEM. Information was also sought from people involved in the different initiatives.

In many cases the information received was about planned activities rather than activities already carried out. These profiles concentrate on what has been done rather than what is planned. It is important from the outset to be aware that there is often a significant gap between plans and achievement. Although this occurs in many areas of development activity, it must be especially factored in when the activity is in an intensely political area where powerful stakeholders, and political events more broadly, often determine what can be achieved and when. This is an important consideration in planning. It should be noted that the profiles were written at the end of 2000 and, in some cases, there may have been developments since then.

These profiles also focus quite narrowly on initiatives that explicitly involve both gender and budgets. There are clearly lessons to be learnt from budget initiatives without a specific gender focus. Nilufer Cagatay *et al.* (2000) discuss some of these lessons in their report of the proceedings of the workshop on pro-poor, gender- and environment-sensitive budgets. There are also lessons to be learnt from gender initiatives that do not specifically focus on the budget. In the confines of this review, however, the gender responsive budgets on their own present sufficient challenge.

Profiles by Region

Africa

BOTSWANA A representative of the United Nations Development Programme (UNDP) in Botswana attended the 1998 Southern African workshop organised by UNIFEM in Harare. Subsequently, together with the Botswana Gender Ministry, UNDP Botswana organised a workshop on gender and budgets for local level planners, researchers and statisticians. This was part of a series of gender sensitisation workshops organised by the Gender Ministry for different groupings. GRB analysis was probably not included in any of the other workshops.

KENYA The Canadian International Development Agency (CIDA) provided funding for a three-year initiative in key Kenyan ministries aimed at mainstreaming gender in public investment plans and recurrent expenditure, gender responsive planning, collecting gender responsive data, developing ministry-specific tool kits and translating the Beijing Platform for Action into a policy matrix. The Collaborative Centre for Gender and Development has played a key role in the exercise. The legal NGO, International Federation of Women Lawyers (FIDA), has also played a role.

University lecturers who are members of the Centre served as consultants and coordinators of the project. The NGO coordinator was a specialist in gender and education and learnt the importance of identifying and networking with specialists from other institutions. Those the project has worked with include planners, economists, analysts, statisticians, researchers and professionals in a variety of disciplines. To date the work has focused on expenditure at the national level. DFID, SIDA and the Royal Netherlands Embassy have expressed interest in funding a further three-year programme that will look in more detail at engendering the national (and perhaps sub-national) budget/s and the Poverty Reduction Strategy Paper (PRSP).

The chosen ministries for the first three years were Agriculture, Health, Education, Public Works, Industrial Development and Local Authority. The entry points were the ministries' gender focal points but the economist planners in target ministries together with a researcher did much of the analytical sectoral work. The list of issues covered suggests that the gender responsive data element focused mainly on internal issues such as participation of women and men in ministries, training opportunities, use of skills, remuneration and benefits. However, the broader analysis is more externally focused.

The Centre and FIDA-Kenya together produced a concept paper entitled 'Translation of the Beijing Platform for Action into the 1998/99 Kenya National Budgetary Process'. Gender trainers from the Centre developed frameworks for engendering the public investment programme (PIP) and ran a half-day workshop for officers responsible for the PIP. The Centre also developed a concept paper on restructuring the civil service, salaries for which account for 80 per cent of the budget in most sectors.

The initiative received strong support from the previous director of planning and current permanent secretary. However, at a lower level already overworked civil servants were often unavailable when the Centre needed them. Another reported obstacle was that the targeted officials had to consult their superiors before they could release information or participate in other ways. There were further difficulties with some senior officials when draft reports were submitted.

Despite these difficulties, in the first year there were already substantial achievements. These included the incorporation of some aspects of the project's concept paper in the 1998 budget and workshops with people from outside government. Later, the Centre lobbied to ensure that a gender expert was seconded to the team responsible for developing the PRSP. As a result gender was identified as one of the thematic areas and the Centre was asked to provide expertise and to house the Nairobi District PRSP secretariat. The Centre is also working with other women's organisations to ensure women's participation at all stages and levels of the PRSP process.

As is clear from the above, activity has not been confined to civil servants. The Centre, together with the women's organisation Friends of Esther and Deborah, organised a workshop on behalf of the Kenya Women's Political Caucus in June 1997 shortly before presentation of the 1997/98 annual budget estimates. In 1998 members of the Women's Political Caucus participated in a post-budget day group analysis of the gender responsiveness of the national budget. Members of the project participated in and distributed materials at the Economic Reform Forums organised by government.

In a separate venture, the Inter-Parliamentary Union organised a regional workshop on 'Parliaments and the budgetary process including from a gender perspective' in Nairobi during May 2000. The workshop was organised in collaboration with UNIFEM and the Commonwealth Parliamentary Association and participants were invited from some 20 countries in Anglophone Africa. Of these countries, at least nine have a GRB initiative of some kind. Marilyn Waring of New Zealand and Mbaye Diouf of the United Nations Economic Commission for Africa (UNECA) dealt with the gender aspects. The regional seminar was preceded by a three-day workshop for Kenyan MPs. The three-day workshop did not specifically focus on gender issues although the summary of proceedings notes that the budget 'should also provide adequately for marginalised groups such as women and the handicapped. Some participants felt this was not currently the case' (Inter-Parliamentary Union, 2000b).

MALAWI CIDA is driving the very new GRB initiative in Malawi. The initial idea was that the initiative should be situated within government, which is CIDA's primary partner in Malawi. The first step was to commission a Malawi Gender Aware Country Economic Report, based on Diane Elson's theory. The next step occurred in August 1999 as part of a multi-donor consultancy on macro financial support to the country. The gender component, although seen as peripheral to the main focus by almost all the agencies, provided the opportunity to test the feasibility of conducting GRB analysis across key ministries through documentary and interview techniques. The report suggested that such analysis was definitely feasible, but that CIDA's initiative should focus on non-governmental rather than government players in the first stages. This recommendation arose from a feeling that introducing yet another donor-driven change in the midst of the many other reforms happening in government at that time would hinder interest and sustainability.

The recommendation received support in further consultations with both NGOs and government. These consultations revealed that neither side felt comfortable about working together. From the government side, as in many other countries, there was some suspicion about NGO intentions. From the NGO side, there was a fear of being stifled and threatened.

The project has been fairly slow to get off the ground, but is still on the agenda. A planning meeting was held in mid-2000 and a shorter, simpler and updated version of the 1999 research has been prepared to popularise the idea. The South African workshop materials (see below) have also been partially adapted for use in planned training activities.

The Ministry of Gender Affairs, Youth and Community Services is very interested in the initiative. Indeed, the recently developed National Gender Policy commits government to developing a GRB initiative. There is interest from players in parliament, including the Finance Committee that had sight of the 1999 report. From the side of the Ministry of Finance there is support for the usual non-gender-specific budget reforms, including public participation in the budget process. To date the main form of public participation appears to be the Budget Breakfasts that occur shortly after the budget is announced. Participants in these breakfasts complain that they serve little real purpose as they occur too late in the process to have an impact.

MAURITIUS In February 2000, UNDP Mauritius organised a workshop on gender responsive budgets for Mauritius, Seychelles, Comoros and Madagascar. The initiative was inspired by the two regional workshops organised by UNIFEM in Harare in late 1998 and late 1999. However, unlike the Southern Africa workshops, participants in the Indian Islands workshop were primarily from government.

In Mauritius, the Ministry of Women, Family Welfare and Child Development took the initiative further. Initial work has been done on four sectoral ministries – Education, Social Security, Health and Agriculture – using the Commonwealth manual method as the basic format. Small teams from each of the ministries compiled draft reports on this work.

MOZAMBIQUE The Swiss Development Corporation provided financial support for the Mozambique initiative. One of the first steps was the translation by Gedlide, a gender NGO, of most of the chapters of the first South African *Women's Budget* book into Portuguese. A second step was the organisation, together with the Ministry of Finance, of a two-day workshop for Finance officials. Organisation of the workshop and subsequent work was greatly facilitated by the fact that the two top officials in the Budget Office were women, and both were keen to integrate gender in the government budget.

After the workshop the head of the Budget Office collected statistics on the numbers of women and men in the public service. These were included in the public documentation for the budget tabled in 1998. In September 1998, the Ministry officials sought to develop a gendered analysis of budgets in four key ministries – Education, Agriculture, Health and Labour. One challenge was the very different levels of detailed and disaggregated data available in different ministries. A second challenge was the very limited information available on donor funding. This problem was particularly serious given that donor funds account for such a large percentage of the government's budget in Mozambique.

At present there appears to be limited activity within government. At least part of the reason lies in the departure of the two top women in the Ministry of Finance. Gedlide has continued to work with civil society. Activities include hosting a seminar with parliamentarians who are members of the Commission on Social Issues, Gender and Environment, and general work on gender within the Ministry of Health at national and provincial level. In 2000 the Ministry of Agriculture and Rural

Development for the first time allocated a specific budget for activities related to gender issues.

NAMIBIA Namibia's Gender Policy of November 1997 states that gender should be integrated into all government policies, processes and programmes. This statement provided the opening for the idea of gender-sensitive budgets. The Swedish International Development Cooperation Agency (SIDA) supported the process on the basis of their existing programme of support to the Namibian Ministry of Finance and the presence of a long-term consultant in the ministry.

The analysis in Namibia focused on two ministries: Education and Culture, and Agriculture, Water and Rural Development. The report also included a chapter on gender and economics which spoke about the shift from women in development (WID) to gender mainstreaming; paid and non-paid work; equality and efficiency; gender and macroeconomics; and gender and state budgets.

The initiative does not appear to have gone further than introducing the concept of gender responsive budgets. However, towards the end of 2000 the Namibian Ministry of Women Affairs and Child Welfare was looking for a consultant to conduct training for around 30 financial advisors in the different ministries and departments of government.

RWANDA Following the establishment of a UNIFEM-supported Gender Desk in the Rwanda Parliament, a seminar on gender responsive budgets was organised. The seminar resulted in specific budget allocations for women's activities in the most recent budget. There has, to date, been no analysis of the extent to which the rest of the budget is gender-sensitive.

SOUTH AFRICA The South African initiatives are closely linked to the end of the apartheid era, and the introduction of a Constitution and ethos that put race and gender discrimination among the most important issues to be tackled. The idea of examining budgets from a gender perspective was raised during the negotiations that preceded the first democratic elections. It was introduced officially when Pregs Govender, one of the more than 100 new women MPs, proposed it during the budget debate that followed soon after the elections in 1994.

The Women's Budget Initiative (WBI) was established in mid-1995. It was a collaborative venture of the Gender and Economic Policy Group of the parliamentary Committee on Finance and two policy-oriented research NGOs. The initiative was seen as non- or extra-governmental on the understanding that MPs are meant to represent civil society and monitor and direct government. The organisers hoped that by linking researchers and MPs, the researchers could be assured that their work would be taken forward into advocacy while the MPs would have a solid basis for their advocacy. In addition, the approach from the start was for the core WBI members to draw in others to participate as researchers and reference people. Further, they did not restrict themselves to economists, but rather promoted an inter-disciplinary approach and as wide as possible spreading of the skills and ideas.

The South African group was aware of the Australian and Canadian initiatives, but drew also on trade union experience of analysing budgets from a worker perspective during apartheid. From the outset, there was a clear policy of integrating gender analysis with an analysis of race, class, geographical area and other axes of disadvantage.

In the first year the initiative was funded through the core funding of one of the NGOs, sourced from the US Agency for International Development (USAID) and Ford Foundation. In subsequent years the Initiative has received support from the Netherlands Embassy, Commonwealth Secretariat, Ford Foundation, UNIFEM, Charles Stewart Mott Foundation, Oxfam-Canada/NOVIB Gender and Development Fund, and GTZ Pilot Project Gender.

In the first year the WBI analysed a limited number of national votes, public sector employment and taxation. The votes were chosen so as to span both social and economic sectors to make the point that there were gender issues everywhere. By the end of the third year all 26 votes of the national budget, as well as some related issues, had been covered. In subsequent years, the analysis extended to local government, donor funding, revenue and intergovernmental relations.

The original research was published as a series of books. A *Money Matters* series then simplified and shortened the material to make it accessible to a second-language speaker with about ten years of education. A set of workshop materials was also developed in order to reach those who seldom read. The WBI developed these materials together with the Gender Education and Training Network. The partners have recently signed a contract with UNIFEM to work with people from other Southern African countries to adapt the materials for regional use.

In addition to the extra-governmental WBI, South Africa served as the first pilot for the Commonwealth Secretariat initiative. For two years, a consultant worked with the Department of Finance preparing gender-related material, which was incorporated in the budget documents tabled on budget day. The Commonwealth Pilot also included some other activities, such as input on gender at meetings, training in one of the provinces and preparation of a discussion on gender responsive budgets. Subsequently, another province independently took up the idea of gender responsive budgeting and organised input for their most senior decision-makers and training for middle-level officials in all departments.

At present, the government initiatives are either dormant or dead. There is a range of reasons for this, some of them not directly related to gender responsive budgets or even gender. However, one of the more direct reasons has been the departure of supportive key players during the early months of 2000.

More generally, possibilities of influencing government are more limited in 2000 than they were in the early years of the new democracy. In another context, Marion Stevens (2000) uses the term 'soft boundaries' to refer to the easy access which South African activists had to people in government and parliament after the 1994 elections given that all had so recently been together in the struggle against apartheid. Several years later the boundaries have hardened, and government itself is no longer so ready to do everything differently. Further, as in many other countries, central government officials are struggling to cope with implementing a number of other new procedures and many have no time for what they see as 'extras'.

The idea of GRB analysis has, however, become quite well known in the country. Some organisations without direct connections to the WBI players have established their own initiatives or called on the WBI to provide assistance. The WBI has also inspired initiatives that look at the impact of the government budget on other groups, such as children and the disabled. One big difference between these initiatives and the WBI is that they employ a simple 'special interest group' argument whereas the WBI argues that it is the conventional approach to economics, and in particular the blindness to the care economy, that is responsible in large part for policy and budgets not being gender responsive.

TANZANIA The Tanzanian GRB activities were initiated by an NGO, the Tanzanian Gender Networking Programme (TGNP). The NGO drew inspiration from both the South African and Australian initiatives. At this stage it is one of the most developed initiatives with activities spanning government and civil society.

Work began in September 1997 at a workshop which brought together TGNP's allies in the other organisations that form part of the Feminist Activism Coalition (FemAct) as well as a few gender activists from government. Over the ensuring years TGNP has undertaken or commissioned research on four national sectoral ministries (Education, Health, Agriculture, and Industries and Commerce), on the central Finance Ministry and Planning Commission, and on the budget process. It has also done some research in selected districts. For most of the sectors TGNP teamed a government official from that sector with a non-governmental researcher. This approach was part of their strategy of reaching key actors, creating openings and building alliances. The findings of the research have been distributed as mimeos and should appear shortly in book form. TGNP has also produced a more popular and shorter version of some of the research in 'Budgeting with a Gender Focus'. The booklet is currently being translated into Kiswahili.

Approximately a year after TGNP embarked on their project, SIDA started funding a parallel exercise in the Ministry of Finance. In 2000, SIDA and the government recognised that TGNP was well placed to act as ongoing consultant to the Ministry in respect of gender responsive budgeting. Six pilot ministries were chosen, many of them matching those in which

TGNP had conducted research. Training workshops and backstopping centred on the newly introduced medium term expenditure framework (MTEF). Budget officials in selected ministries were already receiving general training in how to follow the steps needed for this type of activity. TGNP was invited to attend the initial training. On the basis of that experience they designed and delivered workshops that showed how to integrate gender in each step. This was later formalised into a 'checklist' in response to constant demands for 'tools'.

The collaboration seems set to continue and expand. In October, UK consultants were commissioned by the Ministry of Finance to plan a three-year Public Financial Reform Management Programme which would span all the institutions involved in financial management, not only the budget office. TGNP was commissioned to contribute their gender expertise and found openings for gender-related work in virtually all the institutions concerned. TGNP had also been invited in to related government processes such as the public expenditure review (PER) and the Poverty Reduction Strategy Paper (PRSP).

The relative success of the Tanzanian initiative can be partly explained by TGNP's approach of building alliances from the start. The fact that NGOs and government are now working together is no small feat given past mistrust on both sides. It is particularly remarkable given that the Ministry of Finance is a key player.

One of the problems in Tanzania is the weakness of the budgeting process. The budget office is currently pushing the mtef with some force, and the exercise is extremely detailed. Yet there is some cynicism among budget officials, which can result in a lack of energy in taking the whole exercise, including the gender elements, seriously. Firstly, the country operates according to a cash budgeting system where most Ministries get far less than they have budgeted for in that they are allocated each month only as much as has been collected in revenue. Secondly, there is a sense that the MTEF, alongside performance budgeting, may be yet one more passing fashion imposed by donors and consultants.

TGNP did not plan the current path at the outset. The documents and speeches of the first year speak of the budget initiative more as a lobbying programme situated in civil society. The outside government initiative has, however, encountered some problems. For one thing, the other FemAct partners have tended to leave the initiative to TGNP and to concentrate on their own activities. For another, some gender activists have criticised TGNP for getting too close to government, and for failing to address the larger macro-economic issues.

The potential for cooption was seen from the start. Already in 1998 a TGNP representative reported that 'the strategy is to work together with actors in the government machinery, while keeping a distance so that they do not hijack our agenda and our course of action' (Adelstal, 1998: 6). The success of collaboration to date and TGNP's apparently ability to maintain its independence have persuaded some of the critics that TGNP has chosen the correct path

Another important aspect of the Tanzanian initiative is its recognition that equity is not only about women. The initiative aims for a 'more people-oriented development strategy and equitable allocation of resources'. The materials and approach speak repeatedly about 'women and poor men'.

The Netherlands Embassy funded the initial TGNP initiative. Most of the government work is funded by SIDA. TGNP is now paid for most of its government-related interventions.

UGANDA The Ugandan initiative has been spearheaded by the NGO, Forum for Women in Democracy (FOWODE). FOWODE was established by women MPs and has strong links with the special interest groups caucus in parliament which brings together those occupying reserved seats for women, people with disabilities, youth and workers as well as women who have won 'open' seats. The GRB project started in mid-1997 with input and a practical session at the Women's Caucus meeting to review its first year in parliament. Already at this stage FOWODE had undertaken activities in the area of gender and macroeconomics, for example through training, policy dialogues and the publication of short 'issue briefs'.

Since 1997 FOWODE has commissioned two rounds of research at the national level, as well as a first round of research in two districts. The national research focuses on Education, Health,

Agriculture and the Ministry of Finance and Economic Planning. Gender researchers from Makerere University have done the research with support from reference people from the ministries concerned. This has established a new relationship between activists and government in place of the previous suspicion. The findings have been fed directly back to politicians in the form of issue briefs, memos and papers which have given gender issues 'credibility and respect', rather than having them discussed only as 'sentimental or moral issues' (Byanyima, 2000). The national research will soon also be published as a book. Meanwhile, a simplified version of the first report, 'Sharing the National Cake', is being used by NGOs to spread gender analysis ideas.

The FOWODE initiative has been facilitated by ongoing changes in the government process that attempt to increase inclusiveness and transparency. The process now provides for significant involvement of sector working groups that include civil society representatives. There is widespread acceptance of the need to focus on poverty alleviation and strong attempts to ensure widespread public participation in determining poverty-related objectives. There are also initiatives to increase the decision-making powers of parliamentarians in respect of budgets. However, the draft expenditure estimates and policy recommendations continue to be subject to approval by the World Bank and International Monetary Fund before presentation to cabinet and parliament.

For the research at the local level, FOWODE has, as at national level, gone for an inclusive approach. The workshop that laid the basis for the first research brought together local government officials, MPs, councillors, NGOs and researchers. The district-level research is part of FOWODE's support for women elected at this level. The founders of FOWODE were members of the Constitutional Assembly where they succeeded in achieving a one-third quota for local government. The current support activities are intended to ensure that the women elected have the necessary skills to influence local government decision-making. FOWODE also sees the current moves to decentralise as potentially advantageous to women in that the majority will not, because of poverty and illiteracy, have a direct influence beyond the local level.

FOWODE's training and support provides local councillors with strategic skills to ensure that, while still a minority, they can influence the majority. It also attempts to move them beyond a frame of mind where they see themselves as personally responsible for solving constituents' problems to the realisation that their role is to ensure that government is transparent, accountable and delivers according to citizens' needs. There have been discussions as to whether this training should be women-only or instead include men so as to avoid being 'confrontational'. Overall, FOWODE tends to support women-only or women-dominated training so as to build self-confidence and assertiveness.

In terms of the budget, in the first round of training women councillor participants focused their attention on the women's vote, and a discrete amount of money which many councils set aside for women. In further training FOWODE hopes to move them to see this vote as a 'diversion' and to concentrate instead on looking at the impact of all other expenditures and revenue.

Surprisingly, given the strength of the initiative and the receptive environment, FOWODE experienced some difficulty in obtaining funds. Some of the early work was sponsored by UNDP. The current district level work is supported by DANIDA.

Beyond the FOWODE initiative, the Association of Uganda Professional Women in Agriculture and Environment (AUPWAE) carried out studies on resource allocation at institutional and family level in four sub-national areas. Winrock International Program funded this as part of a broader East African project. Methods included focus group discussions; interviews with representatives of women in local councils, disabled and a few others; secondary data collection; participatory rural appraisal; and other techniques. Further, in October 1999 the Ugandan Debt Network organised a workshop on gender advocacy and budgets that brought together representatives of several NGOs, including FOWODE and AUPWAE.

ZAMBIA The UNIFEM workshop on gender responsive budgets held in Harare in late 1998 was attended by a team of Zambians, primarily from government. Before the workshop the gender machinery discussed the idea with the Ministry of Finance. The process was facilitated by the inclusion in the macroeconomic policy framework of a directive on gender equity in development and poverty alleviation.

Activities since the workshop have included training for gender focal points, planners in sector ministries and women parliamentarians. Outside of government, the NGO Coordinating Committee held a workshop to discuss how gender issues could be addressed in the 2000 budget. At this stage there is a perception on several sides that the key need is for capacity building. The Netherlands Embassy has committed itself to supporting the initiative. The first workshop, planned for early 2001, will focus on the health sector.

ZIMBABWE A team of Zimbabwean researchers was funded as part of the Gender and Economic Reform in Africa (GERA) initiative to conduct GRB analysis. By mid-1999 the team had done preliminary fieldwork in the form of beneficiary assessments in rural and urban communities on the actual and potential benefits people saw from the national budget process. The team was also interested in the 'invisible' transfer of costs imposed by changes in education and health policies. The final report has not yet been submitted to GERA.

Currently the most active player is the Women's Action Group, which has been trying to ensure that gender concerns are considered in the 2001 budgeting process. The Group is particularly concerned about allocations for the health and education sectors. The regional UNIFEM office has been participating in this initiative and one of the UNIFEM staff members presented a paper at the parliamentary pre-budget seminar. The Women's Action Group and the Gender Forum plan to conduct an analysis of the 2001 budget in the hope that this will stimulate a bigger lobby for gender responsiveness in the 2002 budget process. The Gender Forum was initiated by the UN Gender Working Group and provides the opportunity for individuals and representatives of NGOs, government, UN agencies and other donors working on gender and development to discuss current issues and share experiences.

The Americas

BARBADOS Barbados was the third of the Commonwealth Secretariat pilots. One of the important enabling factors in this country was the coordination by a senior level official in the Ministry of Finance. This person spearheaded the initiative in the country. Ultimately, however, his position as secondee could have brought some weaknesses in that he could too easily be labelled as an 'interfering outsider'.

The initiative began with a visit by a Commonwealth delegation to meet with key players. The second step was a workshop in April 1999 involving about three representatives each from the Ministries of Agriculture and Rural Development, Health and Environment, Social Transformation, Education, Youth and Culture, and the Attorney General. The workshop used the basic methodology developed during the Sri Lanka training and reflected in the Commonwealth manual. Participants thus developed the skeletons of reports for each sector on the basis of gender-targeted, employment equity and mainstream expenditures.

Participants were expected to complete their reports after the workshop so as to produce a composite publication. After concerns around time and work pressure, the Commonwealth Secretariat commissioned a Barbadian based in London to complete the report. The final product is a solid piece of research that elaborates at some length on the skeleton produced in the workshop. However, the Attorney General section, which covers the police and thus gender violence, is missing from the report. This is disappointing as it is one of the few exercises to include the policing agency.

The report was written by the consultant, but with support from the ministries. Its tone is fairly academic and probably more attractive to the sophisticated gender analysts in the country than to government officials. There was some attempt to involve or inform gender activists about the initiative, but with limited success. At least one of the activists seemed to think it more useful to engage in this type of analysis within networks such as Development Alternatives with Women for a New Era (DAWN) rather than engaging with government.

BRAZIL Agende, a Brazilian organisation, has worked on policy and budgets with central and federal government in the country, focusing on the ministries of Justice, Health and Work and Employment. The methodology which government uses to formulate budgets has changed over the life of the project. This has added to the usual challenges of budget analysis and has resulted in a special focus on process issues. Agende has not focused specifically on gender, but has raised gender-related issues in the course of its policy and budget analysis.

CANADA In 1993, the Canadian branch of the Women's International League for Peace and Freedom developed a women's budget in celebration of the League's 75the anniversary. The publication is based on five principles, all of which have a clear link with war, the military and defence.

The Canadian government does not have a formal GRB initiative. However, in the early 1990s the Status of Women Canada (SWC) identified the taxation of child support as a gender issue. The institution worked with taxation and family law experts to develop guidelines and options for new policy and consulted with outside groups mobilising around the same issue. Eventually a legal challenge resulted in an official task force. swc itself and outside organisations did not have the data and capacity to model the different options. However, by working with line departments, they were able to come up with a woman-friendly option that was accepted as policy (Karman, 1996: 10-1).

Although it has not consistently focused on gender, the outside government Alternative Federal Budget (AFB) in 1998 included a review of how, analytically and practically, gender could be incorporated in budgets. The review did not examine to what extent the AFB had achieved such integration in the past. The initiative itself acknowledges weaknesses in this respect but notes that there have been 'considerable efforts' to bring in a gender perspective. Thus, one of the eight basic principles underlying the AFB is 'economic equality between men and women' (Loxley, 2000). Up until recently, there was a conscious decision not to have a separate discussion on gender, but rather to insist that it be integrated in other policy sections. There have also been ongoing attempts to ensure that sufficient women participate in the project.

In an attempt to address past weaknesses in respect of gender, AFB is planning the first major steering committee for 2001 to coincide with the National Action Committee on the Status of

Women (NACSW) meeting. The 2001 publication will also, for the first time, include a section that focuses specifically on gender-related issues and proposals.

CHILE Chile has GRB initiatives in both civil society and government. The inside government initiative is coordinated by SERNAM, the country's gender machinery. SERNAM, together with the budget directorate of the treasury and with the assistance of the Inter-American Development Bank, organised a seminar for public servants on mainstreaming gender in projects and programmes. Gender analysis of the budget is planned for 2001.

UNDP is meanwhile supporting a GRB initiative in municipalities in coordination with the regional subsecretary for development. As in other countries, UNDP's initiative was motivated by the increasing powers given to the sub-national level and the hope that this could provide the basis for democratising the relationship between municipalities and the people who live in them. UNIFEM is providing support to a reference group of experts. The work is based on a previous project in 12 communities that utilised four indicators of gender equality: organisation, exercise of rights, social control and access to decision-making and public voice to defend rights. The current initiative is looking at nine municipalities in four regions of the country. The municipalities were chosen on the basis of size, poverty, rurality and existing initiatives around gender equity.

EL SALVADOR Movimiento de Mujeres Melida Amaya Montes, a women's organisation, is working on budget issues in El Salvador.

MEXICO In 1999 a group of women NGO leaders and researchers in Mexico City conducted a study of federal programmes and expenditure in the area of reproductive health. They used the Programme of Action of the International Conference on Population Development (ICPD) as a basis. Subsequently, the NGO Equidad de Genero (Gender Equality) held budget workshops that focused on the needs of poor people. Fundar Centre for Analysis and Research, a relatively new policy research NGO established in January 1999, partnered with Equidad to provide the background research and analysis. By 2000 the two partners had drawn in about 45 women NGO leaders, many of whom wanted to develop similar budget research projects within their own states and municipalities.

Equidad and Fundar have a two-year project plan, funded by the Ford Foundation, to support women leaders in researching and understanding local budgets and using their knowledge in advocacy. The initial phase involves one research team in Mexico City and three teams in states. The project plan provides for a bimonthly email bulletin, two annual public budget workshops and four manuals. The focus will be on both social spending and citizen participation in budgets.

2000 was the first year of the project and was dedicated to research. Advocacy will begin in the later part of the project. During 2000 Fundar was also researching the government's poverty eradication strategy from a gender perspective. In addition, they have started discussions with a government initiative to analyse how public programmes affect women, and hope to work with UNIFEM on building this into the strategy of the government that comes into power in December 2000. The work will include interaction with the statistical bureau.

The National Women's Commission is responsible for a second Mexican initiative, which is located at federal district level. The objective of the programme is to increase awareness among public servants of the administration's responsibilities in respect of inequities resulting from their programming and budgeting processes. While the target is the government, civil society organisations have also participated. As a result of the initiative, the Ministries of Health, Education, Work, Governance, Social Development and Agriculture have signed a convention. A number of programmes and budgets within the different sectors have also been revised.

PERU There are two GRB initiatives in Peru. The first is part of a bigger project on 'Budget transparency for better governance' supported by the Ford Foundation. The gender aspect of this project focuses on the Ministry of Women and Human Development, which is the national machinery for women. A university-based team collected information both from the Ministry of Economics and Finance and from the various institutions that participate in programmes and activities relating to women. Expenditures were classified into different categories: generation of income, literacy, reproductive health and nutrition, gender equality, and institutional development. Other aspects of the overall project focus on environment, youth and defence.

The second project is a pilot being carried out by Centro Flora Tristan with the support of Diakonia and UNIFEM. The project focuses on municipal budgets and is targeted at women councillors in provincial municipalities and districts in urban and rural areas. To date, the initiative has involved 40 municipalities in the coastal, mountain and forest regions of the country.

ST. KITTS AND NEVIS St Kitts and Nevis was the second Commonwealth Secretariat pilot in the Caribbean. It was included to explore practical linkages with the previous work by the government on implementing the Commonwealth gender management system (GMS). One result of the intervention was that the Ministry of Community and Social Development and Gender Affairs was able to argue successfully for a six-fold increase in the allocation for the gender unit.

UNITED STATES OF AMERICA The United States of America (USA) is one of the few countries in the world not to have ratified the Convention on the Elimination of All Forms of Discrimination Against Women (CEDAW). At the sub-national level, several states, counties and cities have passed resolutions urging ratification. San Francisco has gone further by enacting its own ordinance incorporating CEDAW principles. The city's Commission on the Status of Women was given responsibility for implementation with oversight from an eleven-member CEDAW task force that included elected officials, government employees, organised labour and community advocates.

The first step in implementing the new ordinance was to develop a set of guidelines that would assist in gender analysis of two departments for discrimination in respect of employment practices, budget allocation and provision of direct and indirect services (see http://www.ci.sf.uf/cosw/cedaw/guidelines.htm). The Department of Public Works was chosen because of its size, because traditionally it has provided few jobs for women, and because services are provided indirectly rather than to individuals. The Juvenile Probation Department was the second choice as it provides services to an increasing number of women who are also very diverse. The Commission worked with the international consulting group, Strategic Analysis for Gender Equity, in developing the gender analysis guidelines. It completed its first report during 2000. It is currently looking at four more city departments and also at city-wide practices, such as work-life policies and practices.

In a separate initiative, Jane Midgley has done work on women's budgets in the USA and is currently writing *The Women's Guide to the US Budget*.

Asia

BANGLADESH A new GRB initiative, which will be based in a university, is expected to begin in January 2001. The exercise will be conducted in collaboration with the World Bank and will receive funding from both Norway and the Netherlands. The first phase will involve a beneficiary assessment and incidence analysis, to serve as a baseline study. The second phase, planned for around 2003, will involve work with government on a gender-disaggregated budget.

Related, but less overtly labelled as a GRB exercise, the Policy Research Unit in the Ministry of Health in Bangladesh has been doing pilot work linking gender-disaggregated beneficiary assessment with local service delivery. After exploratory discussions, it was agreed that the pilot would focus on three aspects related to delivery of the Essential Package of Services.

The work is being done in the context of the new sector-wide programmes being introduced in Bangladesh as well as many other developing countries. Barbara Evers of Manchester University has acted as consultant in respect of the health sector. At this stage the outputs and targets are linked to donor appraisal processes rather than directly to government processes. Thus while the country is moving – or being pushed – to output budgeting in respect of the full budget, at present this exercise focuses only on donor supported sector programmes. Evers' reports also point to the human resource, computer and other constraints on extending the exercise to the different levels responsible for health delivery.

The health work draws on a beneficiary assessment that took the form of a large sentinel survey of public perceptions of government services intended to serve as a baseline. There were, apparently, some questions raised as to why an international organisation was doing this work when there were competent local institutions. A weakness of the assessment in gender terms is that virtually all respondents were women. Comparison of women's and men's preferences and perceptions is thus impossible. A further weakness of beneficiary assessment more generally is that it usually ignores non-users. Evers suggests that gender-aware analysis would be useful in this respect in identifying gaps in the current approaches to service delivery. Evers' report is also useful in its discussion of how each of the Elson tools (see Annex to Elson article) might be applied in a particular sectoral context (Evers, 1997: 5–6).

INDIA At the local level, the Centre for Budget and Policy Studies and Karnataka Women's Information and Resource Centre (KWIRC) in Bangalore is planning a separate initiative entitled 'Building budgets from below' that is based on KWIRC's previous participatory district level gender audit. The partners have so far formed an association of elected local women politicians in four districts and consulted with 30 organisations around building a coalition. The project proposal explains that the group will work in the areas of (a) skills for planning utilisation of earmarked funds; (b) understanding the existing budget; and (c) drafting a dream budget. The project will, as a first step, look at how to utilise Danish funds that have been allocated for utilisation by rural village women.

There are also some developments within government. In mid-2000 UNIFEM organised a workshop on GRB analysis that was attended by government officials, researchers and gender activists. Since the workshop, the government has agreed that the Department of Women and Child Development, with UNIFEM support, will prepare an annual chapter for the National Economic Survey. A local institute has been commissioned to prepare the chapter with inputs from key gender analysts.

THE PHILIPPINES The Philippines gender and development (GAD) budget, like many others, was inspired by Australia's women's budget. It is probably the most institutionalised initiative after that of Australia. Like Australia's, the initiative is centred inside government and led by the gender machinery in the form of the National Commission on the Role of Filipino Women (NCRFW). But unlike initiatives elsewhere, the GAD budget as introduced in 1996 is very specific as to what is required. It states that every government-related agency must allocate at least five per cent of its budget for gender and development. Proponents were aware of potential criticisms that specifying a percentage as small as five per cent could reinforce women's marginalised access to resources, but proposed a specific amount to avoid vague and immeasurable implementation. The GAD budget was introduced with support from the top, including President Ramos himself.

The GAD budget was seen as a strategic way of ensuring funding for the Philippine Development Plan for Women (PDPW). This Plan should, ideally, have been presented to Congress for approval and allocation of a related budget, but there were fears that Congress was not sufficiently gender-sensitive to give this support. Without the GAD budget, implementation of the Plan would thus have been largely dependent on donor funding. In fact, the first GRB related legislation, Republic Act (RA) 7192 of 1992, specified only that a certain portion of official development assistance was to be spent on women-related programmes and projects. The 1996 measure extended this to all government agencies.

Further developments have subsequently taken place. Since 1998 all agencies have been required to formulate GAD plans and submit these to the ncrfw for approval. NCRFW Management Committee members now sit in on the technical budget hearings conducted by the Department for Budget Management. They also sit in on Congress meetings where agency officials defend their budgets. The GAD budget requirement has also been extended to local government units (LGUs), although there is some controversy as to whether it covers the full budget there or only part of it.

NCRFW monitoring of the GAD budget revealed that in the

early years a large portion of the GAD allocations was spent on women-specific projects responding to practical needs. The second most popular type of allocation was for setting up institutional mechanisms for GAD. The smallest amounts were spent on mainstreaming. Further, while the number of agencies observing the GAD budget requirements has increased over the years, many of the over three hundred national agencies still do not report and even more do not reach the 5 per cent minimum. By 1997 the GAD budgets accounted for less than 1 per cent of total appropriations. The bulk of the amount was accounted for by Health and Agriculture. Finally, some of the allocations are somewhat bizarre, the most notorious relating to ballroom dancing lessons for female officials of the department concerned.

The NCRFW has tried several different ways of assisting agencies to understand what is required, in particular in respect of mainstreaming and ensuring that existing programmes are gender responsive. Some of this work has been funded through CIDA's broader programme of support to the agency. One attempt involved a question-and-answer booklet. The booklet takes a fairly gentle line. It states: 'While activities such as ballroom dancing and livelihood skills training for the agencies' or LGUs' women workers may benefit women, they may not respond to the priority gender issues being addressed by the agencies or LGUs'. A more recent directive that takes a harder line in stipulating unacceptable allocations has reportedly met with some resistance.

Within the NCRFW there is a recognition that the 5 per cent itself is not all that important. The important thing is that the agency should have a GAD plan and see the GAD budget as the means to implement the plan rather than as an end in itself. Ultimately, when the agency's entire operations and budget are gender responsive, they can claim that their GAD budget is 100 per cent.

The NCRFW provides technical assistance to agencies in devising their GAD plans and budgets. It is a larger and stronger organisation than the gender machinery in many other countries. Nevertheless, it is far from large enough to service all the hundreds of central agencies, let alone the LGUs.

In at least some LGUs, women councillors have latched onto the idea and pushed for their own area-specific GRB ordinances. But there are many others where little has happened.

As noted above, the GAD budget is primarily a within-government exercise, although the NCRFW has called on civil society partners for assistance, for example with evaluation. A more recent exercise, initiated by the Asia Foundation, focuses more on civil society. It also focuses on the local level. During the preparatory phase, this exercise was discussed with the NCRFW, who were supportive for a number of reasons. Firstly, by focusing on the local level, the new exercise will provide support where the NCRFW has limited ability to reach. Secondly, the Asia Foundation exercise introduces ideas from GRB exercises elsewhere in the world. It asks what happens to the other 95 per cent of the budget and argues that, until one understand the answer to this, it will be difficult to plan to use the 5 per cent GAD budget effectively. This approach ties in well with the NCRFW's understanding of what the GAD budget is about.

In the first phase the Asia Foundation exercise involved action research in three local governments, plus a background paper discussing the context for gender responsive budgets at local level. Two of the pilot LGUs are ones in which there is a strong woman councillor, based in a local NGO, who has already been active in pushing gender issues. The partner in the third LGU is a people's organisation that has done participatory training around budgets for local officials and citizens. One key aspect of the next phase of the Asia Foundation project will be capacity building around advocacy on the basis of the research findings.

The regional UNIFEM office hopes to work on a parallel initiative with the NCRFW, Department of Budget Management and National Economic Development Authority to investigate possibilities of institutionalising a GRB initiative approach that moves beyond the 5 per cent GAD budget. An initial one-day seminar during June 2000 introduced the '95 per cent' approach to NCRFW and other officials.

SRI LANKA Sri Lanka was the second Commonwealth Secretariat pilot. The choice was useful in illustrating the benefits of a social services-friendly government policy for poorer women and men even where gender is not an explicit aim at the outset. It was agreed that the Ministry of Finance would be the lead agency. The Ministry of Women's Affairs was happy with this position given the resource constraints of their ministry.

Training of government officials took place during April 1998. Participants consisted of a team of officials from Education, Health, Agriculture and Lands, Social Services and Industrial Development. The initiative as a whole was coordinated by the Budget Department of the Ministry of Finance under the leadership of a committed gender activist and economist.

For the Commonwealth team, Sri Lanka served as the testing ground for the approach that was later formalised in the Commonwealth manual. The process included a preliminary mission and capacity building workshop, supported by follow-up visits by the Commonwealth Secretariat. A consultant coordinated the activities of the teams working on the gender analysis of the agriculture, education, health, industry and social services sectors. The final report, prepared by the Department of National Planning, includes special surveys to obtain gender-disaggregated data on service delivery. It focuses on recurrent spending in 1996 but also examines later budgets to a more limited extent. The report also looks at public service employment.

One immediate concrete output of the Commonwealth initiative was specific reference to women's contribution to the economy in the 1999 Budget Speech. Another was the development of a long list of indicators. There was some discussion about introducing the GRB analytical tools into the curriculum of the Sri Lanka Institute of Development and Administration and of introducing gender analysis into appraisal for the Public Investment Programme.

THAILAND The World Bank has initiated a small project in Thailand involving gender analysis of the wid budget within two agencies.

VIETNAM The 1999/2000 Vietnamese public expenditure review coordinated by the World Bank, bilateral donors and the government explicitly gave some attention to gender issues. The Netherlands Embassy played a key role in ensuring that this was done and providing support for the innovation. During the exercise there were ongoing tensions as to what mainstreaming of gender into a PER should entail. The Bank interpreted it as largely confined to the impact of expenditure, particularly in the social sectors. Others argued for a broader analysis that included examination of imbalances at the institutional level. During the research stage there were problems when the 'non-gender' specialists had difficulty in understanding how to incorporate gender into their analysis. Despite these difficulties, the initiative should bring some concrete results as the Bank and Ministry of Finance have agreed on a timetable for implementation of some of the recommendations, including some gender-related ones.

Europe

AUSTRIA Gabriele Michalitsch of the Institut für Volkswirtschaftstheorie und -politik has written articles and conducted lectures and workshops on gender bias in Austria's financial policies, including the national budget. Her work focuses on changes in policy since the take-over of the new government in February 2000.

FRANCE The French government produces a gender impact statement that it issues together with the budget.

GERMANY A small group within Frauenforum, an NGO which is (or was) a member of Women in Development Europe (wide), has been working on gender responsive budgets. A GRB working group of women, mainly from Berlin, was formed in October 2000.

IRELAND Gender impact assessment is incorporated in the implementation of the National Development Plan, which is a multi-year expenditure plan for the period starting in 2000. The government has drawn up gender impact assessment guidelines to guide the exercise.

ITALY In September 2000, the Equal Opportunity Commission of Italy sponsored an international workshop on gender auditing of government budgets. The main sessions focused on experiences in Australia, the United Kingdom, the European Union and three African countries (South Africa, Tanzania and Uganda). The event included a round-table debate with the participation of Italian government authorities and consultants in charge of drafting or analysing budgets at local and national level. It was intended primarily as an opportunity for information-sharing.

NORWAY In Norway the Ministry of Children and Family Welfare has done some gender analysis of the budget.

RUSSIA The Open Society Institute is supporting a GRB initiative.

SCOTLAND After nearly a decade of publishing an annual report on the position of women in Scottish life, the information research and networking organisation, Engender, was invited to a meeting with the Minister of Finance to discuss the relationship between policy and budget. In late 2000, the government agreed to employ someone within the Finance Department to advise government on how to initiate gender impact analysis. Government also agreed to establish a gender advisory group with representation from Engender, other NGOs, the Equal Opportunity Commission, civil servants and politicians.

SPAIN The government of the Basque Country has shown interest in introducing a gender sensitive budget approach. In 2000 there were two initiatives which moved the process forward. The Basque Country's women's office, Emakunde, in partnership with an education information technology company, Infopolis, established a virtual library of materials on gender responsive budgets. These materials are available on the web (www.infopolis.es/usuarios/bibliotec.htm). In addition, Rhonda Sharp was invited to provide a briefing on gender responsive budgets to the President of the Basque Country, his Finance Minister and senior government officials.

SWITZERLAND In March 1994 the trade union of public employees commissioned a study on the direct and indirect impact of cutting the budget deficit on women. The study, published in both full and more popular form (Bauer and Baumann, 1996), was undertaken by a social and labour studies unit and co-financed and co-edited by the trade union and the Swiss Conference of Equal Opportunity Officers (EOO).

The study analysed three issues in respect of public funding:

- Effects on employment of women and men both in the public sector and beyond;
- Effects on women and men as beneficiaries of state services; and
- Effects on non-paid work of women.

The study was disseminated through meeting at cantonal and communal level, within parties and trade unions and at EOO meetings. Since the first study, there has been a range of national, cantonal and communal level initiatives started by women's groups, EOOs, MPs and trade unionists. Basle is most advanced, and the parliament there has instructed the government to take forward the analysis. Motions similar to the Basle one as well as other initiatives exist in Zurich, Aargau and St Gallen.

The Swiss gender responsive budgets are strongest where there is support from progressive political parties and parliamentarians, collaboration with and lobbying by women's organisations, and strong EOOs. The church, and women's groups within the church, have also become advocates of GRB analysis.

One of the problems for Swiss activists in this arena is that the system of budgeting differs between the levels. This has made it more difficult to take the experimental work done at national level to the sub-national level A second challenge is the shift to New Public Management. This shift will change the way budgets are made and drastically reduce the unusually high level of budgetary decision-making power which public representatives and even the general public enjoy in Switzerland. A third problem is the time lag in statistics, which leads to arguments that the research is of no use for policy- or budget-making.

UNITED KINGDOM The key player in the United Kingdom is the extra-governmental Women's Budget Group. This is a loose and small, but impressive, group of gender activists from different sectors. The Group has managed to raise a limited amount of funding, but nothing like the scale of some of the developing country initiatives, and certainly not enough to employ full-time staff.

The Group's potential increased dramatically when the Labour Party was elected in the mid-1990s. This was a result both of personal contacts with those in power and because the new government was more open to addressing disadvantage. It is also more open to consultations, to the extent that it now produces a pre-budget consultation paper in November each year that outlines the main policies and proposed changes. This innovation has allowed the Budget Group and others to make formal submissions that should, theoretically, have more chance of influence (Himmelweit, 2000).

In November 1998 the Treasury and the Women's Budget Group co-hosted a one-day workshop which included inputs on the Canadian, Norwegian and South African experiences of gender-related budget, policy and time use work. Since then, besides submissions at critical points, the Group has had regular meetings with the Treasury.

There is some scepticism within the Group as to whether these meetings really influence the thinking of the Treasury or are rather an opportunity for the Treasury to use them as sounding boards. Yet the Treasury publications, including those issued on budget day, suggest that it is aware of some of the issues, even if not at some of the more profound levels put forward by the Group. For example, Treasury paper 9 of 1998 on 'Women and the Budget' quotes the Chancellor as acknowledging that women predominate in 'workless households, low earners, part-timers, and people with caring responsibilities', all of which 'have often been ignored' (Her Majesty's Treasury, 1998).

The Women's Budget Group's own publications attempt to go deeper in questioning the economic framework implicit in the approach of the Treasury (and general society). So, for example, there is a lot of emphasis on the care economy and on time. The Group's writing, while acknowledging that the government has a stated commitment to poverty eradication, particularly among children and their carers, questions whether this commitment will be honoured if and when it comes into conflict with other policy objectives, such as 'keeping British industry competitive' (Himmelweit, 2000).

The Group focuses on efficiency arguments for gender responsiveness. It argues that these arguments fit well with the Treasury's concern with 'value for money'. It argues, too, that the efficiency argument constitutes a more radical approach than 'fairness' if it is based on an understanding that the concept of 'efficiency' in economic theory needs to be redefined (Himmelweit, 2000).

Unlike many other GRB exercises, the UK one focuses more on taxes and benefits than expenditure. This partly reflects the nature of budgets in the country, in that budget day itself focuses on taxes rather than on spending. Spending is announced later in the year, with very little publicity and public interest. The focus on taxes and benefits also reflects the fact that these affect a far larger proportion of the British population than they do in developing countries.

The Middle East

ISRAEL The Adva Center in Israel conducts analysis of budgets from various angles. It does not have a specific project on gender or women. However, in 1997 the Centre produced an analysis that looked at what the recently released budget meant for women as consumers and as workers. Using this basic framework, the document moves systematically through topics that include health, education child allowances, old age pension, unemployment compensation, labour and social affairs.

LEBANON The regional office of UNIFEM in Beirut recently organised a one-day workshop for UN gender focal points on gender responsive budgeting and auditing.

The Pacific

AUSTRALIA The Australian women's budgets are the longest surviving in the world and were the inspiration for several of the current initiatives. The first Australian women's budget was established in the mid-1980s shortly after the Labour Party came into power. At one stage there were women's budgets at federal level and in each of the territories and states. There are a number of thoughtful assessments of the strengths and weaknesses of the initiatives that are more critical than self-assessments by some other countries, but are useful as pointers to possible weaknesses elsewhere. The following profile draws out only a few of these points.

The Australian women's budgets were situated inside government. They were coordinated by the women's machinery (which would today be called gender machinery or gender management system), but required significant work to be done by all other ministries. The role played by 'femocrats' (feminist bureaucrats) in taking the initiatives forward had both advantages and disadvantages. On the plus side, it was their hard work and commitment that ensured that the work was done and the frameworks developed. On the negative side, their capable management of the process weakened participation by women in civil society. As a result, there were very few complaints when the Women's Budgets were allowed to wither away.

In their heyday, the Australian women's budget statements were thick documents. The Commonwealth (national) document, for example, averaged 300 pages. To attract a wider readership among women's groups, the Commonwealth statement was, however, also issued in a shorter, illustrated format. In most cases the women's documents were released on budget day as official budget documents. Victoria decided to issue their document separately so that it would not be 'lost' among all the other budget information, and so that the Women's Policy Co-ordination Unit, rather than the Office of Management and Budget, could retain more control over the contents (Sawer, 1996: 13).

The documents were thick because they included a comprehensive statement from each ministry and department as to the implications of their expenditure (and sometimes revenue) for women and men. The statements were prepared according to standardised formats that were drawn on in devising the approach suggested in the Commonwealth/AusAID manual (Budlender and Sharp, 1998). Standardised formats are the preferred approach for bureaucratic work, and also ensured that sector officials knew what questions to ask. However, the sheer bulk of the resulting document, and the comprehensive (but boring) standardised format, meant that the reader had to be committed to find all the really useful information they contained. The reader also had to be critical, as few sector officials were likely to criticise their own policies outright, even if they recognised the weaknesses themselves, which many did not. In general the women's machinery officials let the reports stand as prepared by sector officials, 'allowing departments to damn themselves with their own words!' (Sharp and Broomhill, 1990: 6).

A related point is that the documents spoke about what was there in terms of policy and budgets, but did not speak about what had been cut. So, for example, there was no record in the national (Commonwealth) government document of the 1986/87 cuts to the budget of the Human Rights Commission that is the arbitrator for the Commonwealth Sex Discrimination Act (Sharp and Broomhill, 1990: 4).

The women's budget statements have been criticised for being only a reporting or accountability mechanism and thus having no impact on policy. This is perhaps too harsh as it is possible that officials, in compiling the statements, became aware of weaknesses, which they later attempted to correct. There were, however, also more explicit attempts to get gender integrated in policy. For example, in New South Wales the Women's Coordination Unit was given a formal role in the budgetary process that spanned several months of each year. However, Sawer sees even this as being more about finding new initiatives for women than about detailed examination of the gendered effect of all programmes (1996: 14).

In the late 1980s Australia started moving towards programme budgeting. Some femocrats saw this as providing new opportunities for monitoring gender responsiveness. However, by the mid-1990s gender reporting had still not been included among the formal requirements laid down by the Estimates Committee.

With the change in government in the mid-1990s, there was less interest within government to continue the initiatives and some of them were abandoned. The government's diminished gender responsiveness, however, was only one of the reasons for their abandonment. New South Wales, for example, argued that the approach placed too much emphasis on funding and therefore decided to move from gender responsive budgeting to gender auditing. In New South Wales and elsewhere, there was a perception that the returns from the Australian exercises did not warrant the enormous amount of work. This was particularly so given that budgets generally change relatively little from year to year in a stable country situation.

By 1997, only four states' governments still had women's budget exercises. Soon afterwards this dropped to two. One of the factors which protected the two surviving exercises was the presence of stable gender machineries and long-serving top staff (Sharp, 2000). In 2000, however, Tasmania stopped publishing their women's budget statement pending a major review of output budgeting, leaving only the Northern Territory. Unfortunately, the Territory's report is limited, reporting mainly on activities by the Women's Policy Office rather than mainstreamed activities.

More hopefully, with the elections approaching – and perhaps inspired be developments in other countries – the South Australian government is considering re-introducing a women's budget. Even at this stage there is evidence that the previous women's budget statements have left their mark. Thus the seven-page Appendix A of South Australia's Budget Statement for 2000/1 described the impact of the budget on families, while the nine-page Appendix B described the impact on women.

FIJI Fiji was the Pacific pilot for the Commonwealth's Secretariat's programme. Commonwealth support for the Fiji initiative was subsequently postponed following Fiji's suspension from the Councils of the Commonwealth. There is, however, interest on the part of Fiji civil society organisations. In July 2000 the National Council of Women Fiji issued a statement on the mini budget, which bemoaned the lack of gender specific affirmative action as well as the lack of recognition of the need for peace and national reconciliation. Civil society organisations have also made contact with general budget initiatives in other countries.

Composite Bibliography

Ablo, E. and R. Reinikka (1998). 'Do Budgets Really Matter? Evidence from Public Spending on Education and Health in Uganda.' Policy Research Working Paper, World Bank Africa Region, June.

Adelstal, C. (1998). 'Workshop on Mainstreaming a Gender Equality Perspective into Government Budgets.' Report on workshop of 17 December 1997. Swedish International Development Cooperation Agency, Stockholm.

Adva Center (1997). 'How the Proposed 1998 Israel State Budget Will Affect Women.' Tel Aviv.

Alexander, P. with S. Baden (2000). *Glossary on Macroeconomics from a Gender Perspective (Report 48). BRIDGE* in collaboration with GTZ.

Appleton, S. and P. Collier (n.d.). 'On Gender Targeting of Public Transfers'. Mimeo.

Armani, D. (1997). 'Democratising the Allocation of Public Resources: A study of the participatory budget of Porto Alegre, Brazil.' Study commissioned by Christian Aid (UK) as part of the Local Economy Project, Porto Alegre.

Asian Foundation proposal for Democratising Budgets Project, Philippines.

Baden, S. (1997). 'Economic Reform and Poverty: A Gender Analysis' (Report 50). Report prepared for the Gender Equality Unit, Swedish International Development Co-operation Agency.

Bakker, I. (1997). 'Integrating Paid and Unpaid Work into Economic Growth and Human Development Strategies.' Paper for UNDP Workshop on Integrating Paid and Unpaid Work into National Policies, Seoul.

Bauer, T. and B. Bauman (1996). 'An den Frauen Sparen? Auswirkungen der Sparpolitik von Bund, Kantonen und Gemeinden auf die Frauen, Schweizerische.' Konferenza der Gleichstellungsbeauftragten und Schweizerischer Verband des Personals offentlicher Dienste VPOD, Zurich.

Beloe, T. (1998). 'We cannot stop at a mythology of a certain culture. We must be aware and monitor it. Equitable Development: Motivation or Myth.' Dissertation submitted in partial fulfilment of degree requirement, London School of Economics and Political Science, August.

Beneria, L. (1995). 'Towards a greater integration of gender in economics', *World Development*, Vol. 23, No. 11, pp 1839–1850.

Beneria, L. and S. Feldman (eds.) (1992). *Unequal Burden: Economic Crisis, Persistent Poverty and Women's Work.* Westview Press, New York.

Biz/ed / Institute for Fiscal Studies (IFS) Virtual Economy (2001) http://www.bized.ac.uk/virtual/economy/library/glossary/

Blair, H. (2001). 'Civil Society Strategy Assessment for the Philippines.' United States Agency for International Development, Washington, second draft revised.

Brown, L. (1995). 'Gender and the Implementation of Structural Adjustment in Africa: Examining the Micro-Meso-Macro Linkages.' International Food Policy Research Institute, Washington DC.

Budlender, D. (ed.) (1996). *The Women's Budget.* IDASA, Cape Town.

_____ (ed.) (1997). *The Second Women's Budget.* IDASA, Cape Town.

_____ (ed.) (1998). *The Third Women's Budget.* IDASA, Cape Town.

_____ (ed.) (1999). *The Fourth Women's Budget.* IDASA, Cape Town.

_____ (1998). *Men and Women in South Africa.* Central Statistics, Pretoria.

_____ (2000). 'A Review of Gender Responsive Budgets: The Report of a Global Assessment.' Commissioned by the Commonwealth Secretariat, London.

_____ and Sharp, R. with Allen, K. (1998). *How to do a gender-sensitive budget analysis: Contemporary research and practice.* Commonwealth Secretariat and AusAID, London.

Byanyima, W. Input at October 1999 workshop organised by Uganda Debt Network, Kampala

_____ (2000). 'Strengthening Parliamentary Governance through Gender responsive budgeting: The Experience of Three African Countries.' International Workshop on Gender Auditing of Government budget, Commissione Pari Opportunita, Presidenza del Consiglio dei Ministri, Rome.

Cagatay, N., D. Elson and C. Grown (1995). 'Introduction to Gender, Adjustment and Macroeconomics', *World Development*, Vol 23, No 11, pp 1827–1836.

Cagatay, N., M. Keklik, R. Lal and J. Lang (2000). 'Budgets as if People Mattered: Democratising Macroeconomic Policies.' United Nations Development Programme conference paper series, www.UNDP.org/seped/publications/budgets.pdf.

Carr, M. (2000) 'Overview of the Gender responsive budget Work of the United Nations Development Fund for Women (UNIFEM).' Paper presented at the Inter-Agency Workshop on Integrating Gender in Government Budgets, London, 26–27 April.

Centre for Gender and Development (2000) 'Engendering the National Budget and Economic Policies with a special focus on the Public Investment Programme (PIP), the national budget, the poverty reduction strategy paper.' Kenya.

Chiwara, L. (2000) 'Creating a supportive enabling environment for a renewed social contract between government, labour and business cutting across gender lines to ensure a successful private sector initiative for investment and economic growth.' Paper presented at pre-budget seminar for parliamentarians, Harare, 9–10 October.

Commonwealth Secretariat (1989) *Engendering Adjustment for the 1990s. Report of the Commonwealth Expert Group on Women and Structural Adjustment.* Commonwealth Secretariat, London.

_____ (1995) *Commonwealth Plan of Action on Gender and Development.* Commonwealth Secretariat, London.

_____ (1999) *Gender Management Systems Handbook.* Commonwealth Secretariat, London.

_____ (1999) *The Durban Communiqué: Commonwealth Heads of Government Meeting.* Commonwealth Secretariat, London

_____ (2000) *Learning By Sharing: Secretary-General's Report on the Implementation of the Plan of Action.* Commonwealth Secretariat, London.

_____ (2000) 'Report of the Workshop on Improving the Effectiveness of Applying a Gender Analysis to Government Budgets.' Commonwealth Secretariat, London, 26–27 April.

Dalrymple, K. (2000). 'Gender Analysis of the National Budget of Barbados', quoted in 'The Report of the Workshop on Improving the Effectiveness of Applying a Gender Analysis to Government Budgets', Commonwealth Secretariat.

Deardorff, A.V. (2000, 2001). Deardorff's Glossary of International Economics. http://www-personal.umich.edu/ alandear/glossary/

De Bruyn, J. and D. Budlender (1998) 'Intergovernmental fiscal relations' in D Budlender (ed) *The Third Women's Budget.* Institute for Democracry in South Africa: Cape Town.

Demery, L., S. Chao, R. Bemier and K. Mehra (1995). 'The Incidence of Social Spending in Ghana.' PSP Discussion Paper 82, World Bank, Washington DC.

Demery, L. (1998). 'Gender and Public Social Spending: Disaggregating Benefit Incidence.' World Bank Research Paper, Washington, DC.

Department of Finance (1998). 'Medium Term Expenditure Framework: Programme Summary.' Pretoria.

Department of National Planning, Ministry of Finance and Planning (2000). 'Engendering the National Budget of Sri Lanka.' Centre for Women's Research, May.

Dollar, D., R. Fisman and R. Gatti (1999a). 'Are Women Really the Fairer Sex? Corruption and Women in Government.' Policy Research Report on Gender and Development, Working paper series No. 4, The World Bank, Washington, DC, May.

Dollar, D. and R. Gatti (1999b). 'Gender Inequality, income and growth: are good times good for women?' Policy Research Report on Gender and Development, Working paper series No. 1, The World Bank, Washington, DC, May.

Elson, D. (ed.) (1991). *Male Bias in the Development Process*. Manchester University Press, Manchester.

_____ (1999). 'A Tool for Implementing the Platform for Action: Gender-sensitive budget analysis.' Work on Gender, Macroeconomics and Globalisation hosted by the UNDP in partnership with the Ford Foundation, University of Utah and MacArthur Foundation, New York, 25–26 March.

_____ (1999). 'Commonwealth Gender Responsive Budget Initiative: Background papers.' Commonwealth Secretariat, London.

_____ (2000a). 'Gender Budget Initiatives as an Aid to Gender Mainstreaming.' Paper presented at the Ministerial Conference on Gender Mainstreaming, Competitiveness and Growth, OECD, Paris.

_____ (co.) (2000b). *Progress of the World's Women: UNIFEM Biennial Report*. United Nations Development Fund for Women, New York.

_____ and N. Cagatay (1999). 'Engendering Macroeconomic Policy and Budgets for Sustainable Human Development.' Human Development Report Office, United Nations Development Programme, New York.

Esim, S. (1995). *Gender Equity Concerns in Public Expenditure*. World Bank, Washington DC.

_____ (2000). 'Gender-Sensitive Budget Initiatives for Latin America and the Caribbean: A tool for improving accountability and achieving effective policy implementation.' Prepared for the Eighth Regional Conference on Women of Latin America and the Caribbean, Lima, 8–10 February.

_____ (2000). 'Impact of Government Budgets on Poverty and Gender Equality.' Paper prepared for the Workshop on Improving the Effectiveness of Applying a Gender Analysis to Government Budgets, Commonwealth Secretariat.

Evers, B. (1997). 'Strengthening Gender Awareness in the Bangladesh Health Sector.' Final Report on visit to Dhaka 4–17 May 1997.

_____ (1999a). 'Assessment of the Health Sector Expenditure Formats for Gender and Equity Sensitivity Information and Analysis.' Ministry of Health and Family Welfare, Bangladesh. Part II.

_____ (1999b). 'Assessment of Health Sector Expenditure Formats for Gender and Equity Sensitive Information and Analysis in MOHFW.' Final Report.

Falk, S. and I. Shapiro (1999). 'A Guide to Budget Work: A Systematic Overview of the Different Aspects of Effective Budget Analysis.' The International Budget Project. Centre on Budget and Policy Priorities, Washington.

FUNDAR and Equidad de Genero (1999) 'Women Leaders Getting In: Advocacy skills building for gender-sensitive public spending.' San Angel.

Gender Advocacy Programme (2000). *Making the Act Work: A Research Study into Budgetary Allocations for the Implementation of the Domestic Violence Act*. GAP, Cape Town.

Glover, D. (1993). 'Policy Researchers and Policy Makers: Never the Twain Shall Meet.' http://www.IDRC.org.sg/eepsea/paper/policy.htm.

Goetz, A.M. (1994). 'From feminist knowledge to data for development: The bureaucratic management of information on women and development', *IDS bulletin* 25(2):27–36.

_____ (1995). 'The Politics of Integrating Gender to State Development Processes: Trends, Opportunities and Constraints in Bangladesh, Chile, Jamaica, Mali, Morocco and Uganda.' UNRISD Occasional Paper 2, Geneva, May.

Govender, P. (1995). Joint Standing Committee on Finance Budget Workshop, 13 November.

Government of South Australia (2000). 'Budget Statement 2000–2001.' Budget Paper 2, Adelaide.

Government of Tanzania (2000). 'Status Report on Integrating Gender into the National Budgetary Process in Tanzania.' Prepared for Sixth Meeting of Commonwealth Ministers Responsible for Women's Affairs, New Delhi, 16–19 April.

Grown, C., D. Elson and N. Cagatay (July 2000). 'Introduction' in *World Development* Vol. 28 No. 7, pp 1146.

Haddad, L, L.R. Brown, A. Richter and L. Smith (1995). 'The Gender Dimensions of Economic Adjustment Policies: Potential Interactions and Evidence to Date.' *World Development*, Vol 23, No 6, pp 881–896.

Hannan, C. (2000). 'Gender Mainstreaming in Economic Development in the United Nations.' Paper presented at the Ministerial Conference on Gender Mainstreaming, Competitiveness and Growth, OECD, (November 2000) Paris.

Her Majesty's Treasury (1998). 'Budget 98: New Ambitions for Britain.'

Hewitt, G. (2000a). 'Incorporating Gender into National Budgets: An Overview of Commonwealth Experiences.' Paper prepared for the Workshop on Improving the Effectiveness of Applying a Gender Analysis to Government Budgets, Commonwealth Secretariat.

______. (2000b). 'Applied Gender Analysis to Government Budgets: A South African Example.' Paper presented at the Ministerial Conference on Gender Mainstreaming, Competitiveness and Growth, OECD, Paris.

______ and S. Raju (1999). 'Commonwealth Gender Responsive Budget Initiative (programme overview).' Commonwealth Secretariat, London.

______ and S. Raju (2000). 'Strengthening Economic Governance: Applied Gender Analysis to Government Budgets.' Working paper, Commonwealth Secretariat, London.

Hill, A. and E. King (1995). 'Women's Education and Economic Well-Being', *Feminist Economics*, Vol 1 No 2, pp 21 46.

Himmelweit, S. (2000). 'The Experience of UK Women's Budget Group.' Paper prepared for the Workshop on Improving the Effectiveness of Applying a Gender Analysis to Government Budgets, Commonwealth Secretariat.

Hoima District Budget Speech, Uganda.

Honculada, J.A. and R. Pineda-Ofreneo (2000). *Transforming the Mainstream: Building a gender-responsive bureaucracy in the Philippines 1975–1998*. UNIFEM, Bangkok.

International Budget Project, The (2000). 'A Taste of Success: Examples of the Budget Work of NGOs.' Centre on Budget and Policy Priorities, Washington, October.

Inter-parliamentary Union (2000a). 'Summary of the proceedings of the ipu seminar for the national assembly of Kenya on Parliament and the Budget Process, 18–19 May 2000.'

______ (2000b). 'Results of the Regional Seminar on Parliament and the Budgetary Process including from a Gender Perspective, Nairobi 22–4 May.'

Jayamaha, R. (1998). 'Gender and National Budget Initiative Sri Lanka: Summary of project evaluation meetings held in the Ministry of Finance. Commonwealth Secretariat, London.

_____ and G. Hewitt (2000). 'Building a European Network of Women's Budget Groups: Commonwealth Experience.' Paper prepared for the International Workshop on Gender Auditing of Government Budgets, Rome, 15–6 September.

Jenkins, R. and A.M. Goetz (1999). 'Accounts and Accountability: Theoretical Implications of the Right-to-Information Movement in India' in *Third World Quarterly* 20(3): 603–622.

Karman, Z.E. (1996). 'Feminist Initiatives to gender macro-economic policies in Canada.' Paper prepared for the UNRISD/CPD workshop Working Towards a More Gender Equitable Macro-Economic Agenda, Rajendrapur, 26–8 November.

Kaul, I., I. Grunberg and M. Stern (1999). *Global Public Goods.* Oxford University Press, Oxford.

Klasen, S. (1999). 'Does gender inequality reduce growth and development? Evidence from cross-country regressions.' Policy Research Report on Gender and Development, Working paper series No. 7, The World Bank, Washington, DC.

Krafchik, W. and J. Wehner (1999). 'The Role of Parliament in the Budget Process. Institute for Democracy in South Africa' in *South African Journal of Economics*, December.

Krug, B. and I. van Staveren (1999). 'Gender Audit: Whim or Voice?' Draft for publication in *Public Finance and Gender.*

Kuteesa, F. (1999). 'Central Government Budget Cycle.' Presentation at Advocacy Training Workshop on Budgeting Policy Formulation, October.

Local Government Development Support Programme (1999). Report of the GPC workshop: How to conduct a gender-sensitive budget analysis, Kimberley, 13 April.

Loxley, J. (1999). 'The Alternative Federal Budget in Canada: A New approach to Fiscal Democracy.' Paper prepared for Pro-Poor, Gender- and Environment-Sensitive Budgets, New York, 28–30 June.

_____ (2000). 'Political and Policy Considerations in Alternative Budgets: The Alternative Federal Budget in Canada.' Paper prepared for the Inter-Agency Workshop on Improving the Effectiveness of Integrating Gender into Government Budgets, London, 26–7 April.

Madorin, M. (1999). 'Engendering Budgets in Switzerland: An analysis of new initiatives.' Paper prepared for Pro-Poor, Gender- and Environment-Sensitive Budgets, New York, 28–30 June.

March, C. (1999). 'Gender means doing things differently: Lessons from Oxfam's Women's Linking Project' in Porter, F., I. Smyth and C. Sweetman *Gender Works: Oxfam Experience in Policy and Practice*. Oxfam: Oxford: 259–70.

MBM Change Agents (1997). A Review of Ford Foundation Grants relating to Gender and Public Policy. Draft.

McGee, R. with A. Norton (2000). 'Participation in Poverty Reduction Strategies: A synthesis of experience with participatory approaches to policy design, implementation and monitoring.' IDS Working Paper 109.

Monsod, T. (1999). 'Budgeting for GAD: A Review and Refocusing.' Produced for WAND, Manila

Mauritius Ministry of Finance (2000). Keynote Address by the Minister of Finance at the Opening of the Regional Workshop on Engendering Budgets. Mimeo, February 2000.

OECD (2000). Ministerial Conference on Gender Mainstreaming, Competitiveness and Growth, background document, OECD, Paris, November.

Palmer, I. (1991). *Gender and Population Adjustment of African Economies: Planning for Change*. ILO, Geneva.

______ (July 1995). 'Public Finance from a Gender Perspective' in *World Development* Vol. 23 No. 11, pp 1981.

Pearson, R. (1995). 'Bringing It All Back Home: Integrating Training for Gender Specialists and Economic Planners' in *World Development* 23(11):1995–1999.

Porter, F. and I. Smyth (1999). 'Gender training for policy implementers' in Porter, F., I. Smyth and C. Sweetman *Gender Works: Oxfam Experience in Policy and Practice*. Oxfam: Oxford: 326–333.

Programme of Work for the Ad Hoc committee on the Qualify of Life and Status of Women – 1997 and 1998, South African Parliament.

Razavi, S. (1997). 'Working towards a more gender equitable macro-economic agenda.' Report of the UNRISD/CPD workshop, Rajendrapur, 26–8 November 1996.

Reeves, H. and H. Wach (1999). 'Women's and gender responsive budgets: an annotated resource list.' Prepared for the Swedish International Development Cooperation Agency.

Report and recommendations to Ministers on exploratory discussions regarding the South Africa/Commonwealth Gender and Macro-economic Policy Pilot Study.

St Hill, D. (2000). 'Gender Analysis of the National Budget of Barbados: 1998–1999 (draft).' Project report prepared for the Commonwealth Secretariat, London.

Saito, K. and D. Spurling (1992). 'Developing Agricultural Extension for Women Farmers.' World Bank Discussion Paper 156, Washington DC.

Sawer, M. (1990). *Sisters in Suits: Women and Public Policy in Australia*. Allen and Unwin, Australia.

_____ (1996). 'Feminist Initiatives to Gender Macro-Economic Policies in Australia.' Paper presented to the United Nations Research Institute for Social Development Conference, Rajendrapur, 26–8 November.

Schick, A. (2000). 'The Changing Role of the Central Budget Office' in *OECD Journal of Budgeting*, Vol. 1 No. 1.

Sen, G. (1999). *Gender Mainstreaming in Finance*, Commonwealth Secretariat, London

_____ and C. Grown (1988). *Development, Crisis and Alternative Visions*. Earthscan Publications, London.

Senapaty, M. (2000). 'Workshop on Gender responsive budgets.' Report of workshop organised by UNIFEM South Asia Regional Office, New Delhi, 10 July 2000.

Sharp, R. and R. Broomhill (1990). 'Women and Government Budgets' in *Australian Journal of Social Issues*, Vol. 25, No.1

_____ (1999). 'Australia's role in the development of gender-sensitive budgets.' Paper presented at the UNDP and UNIFEM Workshop on Pro-Poor, Gender and Environment-Sensitive Budgets, UNDP, New York, 28–30 June.

Sharp, R. (1999). 'Women's Budgets' in Peterson, J. and M. Lewis (eds.) *The Elgar Companion to Feminist Economics*. Edward Elgar, New York.

_____ (2000). 'Gender responsive budgets: The Australian Experience.' Paper prepared for the International Workshop on Gender Auditing of Government Budgets, Rome, 15–6 September.

Simkins, C. (1997). 'An academic applied economist looks at the medium term expenditure framework'. Mimeo. Johannesburg.

South Africa (2000). Report of the parliamentary delegation to the Beijing+5 conference. New York 2–9 June.

Sri Lanka Ministry of Finance and Planning (2000). *Engendering the National Budget of Sri Lanka*. Centre for Women's Research, Colombo.

Stark, A. and S. de Vylder (1998). 'Mainstreaming Gender in Namibia's National Budget.' Prepared on behalf of Department of Women's Affairs and Ministry of Finance.

Stevens, M. (2000). 'Abortion reform in South Africa' in *Initiatives in Reproductive Health Policy*, July: 4–6.

Stiglitz, J.E. (1996). 'The Role of Government in Economic Development' in Bruno, M. and B. Pleskovic (ed.) *Annual World Bank Conference on Development Economics*. The World Bank, Washington DC.

Stotsky, J. (1996). 'Gender Bias in Tax Systems.' IMF Working Paper, IMF, Washington DC.

Tanzania Ministry Responsible for Women's Affairs (2000). 'Status Report on Integrating Gender into the National Budgetary Process in Tanzania.' Paper prepared for Sixth Meeting of Commonwealth Ministers Responsible for Women's Affairs, New Delhi, 16–19 April.

Tanzania Gender Networking Programme (1999). *Budgeting with a Gender Focus*. TGNP, Dar es Salaam.

Taylor, V. (1999). *Gender Mainstreaming in Development Planning*. Commonwealth Secretariat, London.

Tibaijuka, A. (1994). 'The Cost of Differential Gender Roles in African Agriculture: A Case Study of Smallholder Banana-Coffee Farms in the Kagera Region, Tanzania', *Journal of Agricultural Economics*, Vol 45, No 1, pp 69–81.

Tzannatos, Z. (1991). 'Potential Gains from the Elimination of Gender Differentials in the Labour Market' in G. Psacharopoulos and Z. Tzannatos (eds) *Women's Employment and Pay in Latin America, Report No 10*. Latin America and Caribbean Technical Department, World Bank, Washington DC.

UNIFEM (1998). 'Engendering the Ninth Five-Year Plan of India, 1997–2000: Report of the Process.' New Delhi.

_____ (1999). Capacity Building for Gender responsive budgets in Southern Africa: A UNIFEM regional training workshop. Harare, 17–19 November.

_____ (2000). 'Strengthening Economic governance: Applied Gender Analysis to Government Budgets.' Concept paper submitted to the Belgium State Secretary for Development Cooperation, New York.

UNRISD (1997). 'Gender, Poverty and Well Being: Indicators and Strategies.' Background note and project proposal, Geneva.

Waring, M (1988). *If Women Counted: a New Feminist Economics*, Harper and Row, New York.

Watt, P. (2000). *Social Investment and Economic Growth: A Strategy to Eradicate Poverty.* Oxfam Publication, UK.

Women's Budget Group, The (1998). 'The Purse or the Wallet?' Proceedings of a seminar held on 12the February 1998, London.

Women's Budget Initiative (1996). 'Report of Women's Budget Initiative Workshop.' Cape Town.

Women's International League for Peace and Freedom, Ottawa Branch (1993) 'The Canadian Women's Budget.' Ottawa.

_____ (February 1996) 'Women's Budget.' Special Edition. Philadelphia, Washington, Arlington.

World Bank (1994). *Zambia Poverty Assessment.* World Bank, Washington DC.

_____ (1995). *Toward Gender Equality: The Role of Public Policy.* World Bank, Washington DC.

_____ (1998). *Public Expenditure Management Handbook.* PREM Network, World Bank, Washington DC.

World Bank Group. 'Public Spending for Equity: The Distributional Dimension.' Topic brief, www1.worldbank.org/publicsector/pe/spending.htm

World Development Journal. Special Issues on Gender and Economics, Vol. 23 (11), 1995 and Vol. 28 (7), 2000, Pergamon, UK.

Yilmaz, S. (2001). 'Concept of Fiscal Decentralization and Worldwide Overview.' UNDP working paper, New York.

Glossary of Terms

Aggregate demand The total demand for a country's output, including demands for consumption, investment, government purchases, and net exports.

Aggregation The combining of two or more kinds of an economic entity into a single category. Data on international trade necessarily aggregate goods and services into manageable groups. For macroeconomic purposes, all goods and services are usually aggregated into just one.

Balance of payments The balance of payments accounts record all a country's international transactions. The sale of exports and national investments by other countries are entered as a credit, while purchasing imports or national companies investing abroad are entered as a debit. The overall account is called the balance of payments because the total of outflows is supposed to be equivalent to (balance) the total of inflows.

Budget The budget is the annual announcement of the government's fiscal policy changes. It announces the tax changes proposed for the following tax year, and also how the government plans to spend that revenue.

Budget deficit When government expenditure exceeds government income.

Budget surplus When government income exceeds government expenditure.

Crowding out A situation in which the government is borrowing heavily while businesses and individuals also want to borrow. The former can always pay the market interest rate, but the latter cannot, and is crowded out.

Depreciation A fall in the value of a country's currency on the exchange market, relative either to a particular other currency or to a weighted average of other currencies. The opposite of 'appreciation'.

Exchange rate The price at which one country's currency trades for another, typically on the exchange market.

Exchange rate regime The rules under which a country's exchange rate is determined, especially the way the monetary or other government authorities do or do not intervene in the exchange market. Regimes include floating exchange rates, pegged exchange rate, managed float, crawling peg, currency board and exchange controls.

False economies A 'false economy' is where an attempt to reduce or contain financial costs in one sector in fact transfers or perpetuates actual costs in terms of time use for individuals and groups, and lowers their overall productivity. Hence there are no actual savings for these individuals and groups, particularly women

Fiscal policy The use by a government of its expenditures on goods and services and/or tax collections to try to influence the nation's level of economic activity. The government can cut taxes and increase government expenditure to encourage more spending and boost the economy (expansionary or reflationary policy) or increase taxes and cut expenditure to reduce the level of demand in the economy and help to reduce inflation (contractionary or deflationary policy).

Gender The notion of gender as distinct from sex refers to the socially constructed roles and socially learnt behaviour and expectations associated with males and females. Women and men differ biologically, but all cultures interpret and elaborate these innate biological differences into a set of social expectations of what behaviours and activities are appropriate and, consequently, what rights, resources and powers men and women possess. While societies vary in terms of their expectations from women and men, they nonetheless all have gender asymmetries that are deeply entrenched (though not static).

Gender-blindness means ignoring the different socially determined roles, responsibilities, and capabilities of men and women. Gender-blind policies are based on information derived from men's activities and/or assume those affected by the policy have the same (male) needs and interests.

Gender-disaggregated data Identifying and generating gender statistics is a complex process, which extends beyond the simple disaggregation of indicators into the categories of women and men. Gender-disaggregated data focus on issues of particular relevance to women and men, girls and boys, and their different roles and positions in society. Statistics on household distance from water or fuel, for example, have different implications for women and men since it is usually the former who spend time collecting these necessities when they are not readily available.

Gender focal point A Gender Focal Point is a designated member of staff in an organisation, ministry, department or division who is the main agent for facilitating, on a day-to-day basis, the integration of gender issues into the policies, programme and projects being undertaken within the institutional structure.

Gender mainstreaming 'Mainstreaming a gender perspective is the process of assessing the implications for women and men of any planned action, including legislation, policies or programmes, in any area and at all levels. It is a strategy for making women's as well as men's concerns and experiences an integral dimension in the design, implementation, monitoring and evaluation of policies and programmes in all political, economic and societal spheres so that women and men benefit equally and inequality is not perpetuated. The ultimate goal is to achieve gender equality.' (Agreed conclusions of the UN Economic and Social Council 1997/2).

Gender management system (GMS) The GMS is an integrated network of structures, mechanisms and processes put in place in an existing organisational framework in order to guide, plan, monitor and evaluate the process of mainstreaming gender into all areas of an organisation's work. It is intended to advance gender equality and equity through promoting political will; forging a partnership of stakeholders including government, private sector and civil society; building capacity; and sharing good practice. The Commonwealth Secretariat is encouraging the establishment of gender management systems at the national level.

Gender neutral Gender neutral policies are not specifically aimed at either men or women and are assumed to affect both sexes equally. However, they may actually be gender-blind (see above).

Gender responsive budget (GRB) GRB is increasingly being adopted as the name for a variety of processes and tools such as a 'gender sensitive budget', 'gender budget', 'women's budget' and 'women's budget statement'. These processes aim to assess the impact of government budgets, mainly at national level, on different groups of men and women, through recognising the ways in which gender relations underpin society and the economy. Although the focus of these exercises has been on determining the impact of budget expenditure on women and girls, they are not separate budgets for women. They include analysis of gender targeted allocations (e.g. special programmes targeting women); they disaggregate by gender the impact of mainstream expenditures across all sectors and services; and they review equal opportunities policies and allocations within government services.

Good governance While good governance is defined in different ways, it is primarily considered to be a process of improving opportunities for the delivery of goods and services to the people in a fair, just, effective and responsible way. Key features are transparency, accountability and participation.

Gross domestic product (GDP) The market value of all final goods and services produced in a given time period, usually a year.

Gross national product (GNP) The market value of all final goods and services produced by national residents, no matter where they are located.

Inflation A general rise in the average level of all prices. It can be measured either monthly, quarterly or annually.

Macroeconomics The study of the behaviour of the overall economy, including inflation, unemployment and industrial production. It focuses on the level of income or output of the economy, including the level of employment, aggregate investment, total consumption and the money supply.

Microeconomics The study of the behaviour of small economic units, such as that of individual consumers, households or companies. It focuses on the determination of the prices that induce these agents to act, including wages for labour and return rates of investment funds. These concerns cover issues of demand and supply, welfare and distribution.

Monetary policy Monetary policy is the control of the money supply and interest rates by a government in order to achieve its economic objectives, in particular the restraining of inflation.

Non-governmental organisations (NGOs) An NGO is any non-profit, voluntary citizens' group which is organised on a local, national or international level. NGOs perform a variety of services and humanitarian functions, bring citizens' concerns to governments, monitor policies and encourage political participation at the community level. Some are organised around specific issues, such as human rights, the environment or health.

Reproductive sector The reproductive sector is concerned with caring for the present and future labour force, and the human population as a whole, including providing food, clothing and shelter in the household. Elson refers to it as the 'care economy'. The reproductive sector is generally unpaid and usually excluded from national accounts. Reproductive labour is mainly performed by women, and takes up an extremely high proportion of their time allocation.

Stabilisation policy The use of monetary and fiscal policies to stabilise GDP, aggregate employment and prices.

Stabilise To reduce the size of fluctuations in an economic variable over time. Examples include stabilising exchange rates by exchange market intervention, stabilising the price of a commodity by operation of a buffer stock and stabilising GDP by macroeconomic stabilisation policy.

Structural adjustment programmes (SAPs) SAPs are intended to restore a sustainable balance of payments, reduce inflation and create the conditions for sustainable growth in per capita income. Typical measures are spending cuts in the public sector and tight monetary policy. At least 75 developing countries undertook SAPs in the 1980s, with loans from the World Bank and IMF. It has been argued that these policies have a disproportionate effect on women because they fail to take into account women's roles in the reproductive sector, the gender division of labour and inequalities in household allocations.

Supply response The increase in output as a result of changed incentives. There a variety of gender-related reasons that affect women's willingness, or ability, to increase their output, or to market their increased output. These include the burden of household work, lack of control over productive resources such as land and the fact that women may not receive the benefits of their own increased production.

Time budgets Also called 'time use studies' and 'time allocation studies', time budgets are used to investigate the allocation of time among different tasks (and leisure). Time budget surveys have revealed the failure of conventional labour statistics to capture the extent, range and complexity of activities in which individuals engage, particularly in developing countries and particularly among women, for whom multi-tasking is common.

Sources: Alexander, P. with S. Baden (2000); Baden, S. (1997); Biz/ed / Institute for Fiscal Studies (2001); Deardorff, A.V. (2000/2001); Elson, D. (1995); Sharp (1999) Institut für Volkswirtschaftstheorie und Politik.